To the Reader:

Scientology® applied religious philosophy contains pastoral counseling procedures intended to assist an individual to gain greater knowledge of self. The mission of the Church of Scientology is a simple one: to help the individual achieve greater self-confidence and personal integrity, thereby enabling him to really trust and respect himself and his fellow man. The attainment of the benefits and goals of Scientology philosophy requires each individual's dedicated participation, as only through his own efforts can he achieve these.

This book is part of the religious literature and works of the Scientology Founder, L. Ron Hubbard. It is presented to the reader as a part of the record of his personal research into life, and the application of same by others, and should be construed only as a written report of such research and not as a statement of claims made by the Church or the Founder.

Scientology philosophy and its forerunner, Dianetics® spiritual healing technology, as practiced by the Church, address only the "thetan" (spirit). Although the Church, as are all churches, is free to engage in spiritual healing, it does not, as its primary goal is increased spiritual awareness for all. For this reason, the Church does not wish to accept individuals who desire treatment of physical or mental illness but prefers to refer these to qualified specialists of other organizations who deal in these matters.

The Hubbard® Electrometer is a religious artifact used in the Church confessional. It in itself does nothing, and is used by ministers only, to assist parishioners in locating areas of spiritual distress or travail.

We hope the reading of this book is only the first stage of a personal voyage of discovery into this new and vital world religion.

Church of Scientology International

This Book Belongs to:

_____

_____

(Date)

DIANETICS 55!

L. RON HUBBARD

DIANETICS 55!

A Guide to Effective Communication

Bridge

PUBLICATIONS, INC.

Published in the U.S.A. by
Bridge Publications, Inc.
4751 Fountain Avenue
Los Angeles, California 90029

ISBN 0-88404-417-3

Published in other countries by
New Era Publications International, ApS
Store Kongensgade 55
1264 Copenhagen K, Denmark

ISBN 87-7336-600-5

Library of Congress No. 73-184345

Printed in the United States of America

Dianetics spiritual healing technology is man's most advanced school of the mind. *Dianetics* means "through the soul" (from Greek *dia*, through, and *noos*, soul). *Dianetics* is further defined as "what the soul is doing to the body." It is a way of handling the energy of which life is made in such a way as to bring about a greater efficiency in the organism and in the spiritual life of the individual.

Important Note

In reading this book, be very certain you never go past a word you do not fully understand.

The only reason a person gives up a study or becomes confused or unable to learn is because he or she has gone past a word that was not understood.

The confusion or inability to grasp or learn comes AFTER a word that the person did not have defined and understood.

Have you ever had the experience of coming to the end of a page and realizing you didn't know what you had read? Well, somewhere earlier on that page you went past a word that you had no definition for or an incorrect definition for.

Here's an example. "It was found that when the crepuscule arrived the children were quieter and when it was not present, they were much livelier." You see what happens. You think you don't understand the whole idea, but the inability to understand came entirely from the one word you could not define, *crepuscule,* which means twilight or darkness.

It may not only be the new and unusual words that you will have to look up. Some commonly used words can often be misdefined and so cause confusion.

This datum about not going past an undefined word is the most important fact in the whole subject of study. Every subject you have taken up and abandoned had its words which you failed to get defined.

Therefore, in studying this book be very, very certain you never go past a word you do not fully understand. If the material becomes confusing or you can't seem to grasp it, there will be a word just earlier that you have not understood. Don't go any further, but go back to BEFORE you got into trouble, find the misunderstood word and get it defined.

Definitions

As an aid to the reader, words most likely to be misunderstood have been defined in footnotes the first time they occur in the text. Words sometimes have several meanings. The footnote definitions in this book only give the meaning that the word has as it is used in the text. Other definitions for the word can be found in a dictionary.

A glossary including all the footnote definitions is at the back of this book. This glossary is not meant as a substitute for a dictionary.

The *Dianetics and Scientology Technical Dictionary* and *Modern Management Technology Defined* are both invaluable tools for the student. They are available from your nearest Scientology church or mission, or directly from the publisher.

Contents

Preface

*S*ecret! Secrets, secrets, *secrets!* Ah, the endless quest, the far, far search, the codes, the vias, the symbols, the complications, the compilations, the mathematicity[1] and abstractacity[2] of secrets, secrets, secrets.

And truth. *Truth!* From Keats[3] to Johnny Jones, we all have traffic with the truth, truth, *truth!* The professors have a truth, the religionists have a truth, the stars and almost anything but government have a truth, truth, *truth.*

Knowledge! Endeared as a precious torch, abhorred as a neurotic's nightmare, it is all knowledge, knowledge, *knowledge!* You get diplomas for it and buy books full of it, you perish for the lack of it or triumph in the absence of it, but whatever it might be, knowledge is precious, dangerous, valueless and horrible and craved.

And what is *knowledge?* And what is the *secret?* And what is *truth?*

---

1. **mathematicity:** the state or condition of being mathematical.

2. **abstractacity:** quality of being difficult to understand.

3. **Keats:** John Keats (1795–1821), English poet, considered one of the greatest English poets. His poems are unequaled for dignity, melody and richness of imagery.

Pontius Pilate[4] asked the question when he washed his hands. Alexander[5] executed messengers when the truth was unpalatable. The Chaldean[6] priest corralled a bit of truth and ruled Chaldea into yesterday and Babylon[7] into dust motes. And rulers and men, scholars and generals have condemned with it, dedicated their lives to it, fought for it and denied it and—have never defined it.

What is *truth?* What is *knowledge?* What is the *secret?* Are they inventions from a shaman's[8] dream? Are they connected with science? Do they belong to philosophy? What are they, whence do they come? Do they exist? Are they owned? Have they ever been written or spoken or guessed? And would one go mad if he knew them?

Dianetics moved into the world on May 9, 1950, with the publication of a book, *Dianetics: The Modern Science of Mental Health*. It moved with violence although its message was peace. A half a million Americans read it, many, many of these acted upon it and are still acting upon it, and every year it sells still more copies—more copies than the average "best seller."

Dianetics was an adventure into the dark realms of the

---

4. **Pilate, Pontius:** first century A.D. Roman prosecutor who condemned Jesus to be crucified. According to the Bible he attempted to not be responsible for Jesus' death by publicly washing his hands and giving responsibility to a mob of people who were calling for Jesus' death.

5. **Alexander:** Alexander III (356–23 B.C.), also known as Alexander the Great, king of Macedonia, an ancient kingdom located in what is now Greece and Yugoslavia.

6. **Chaldean:** of Chaldea, an ancient province of Babylonia, approximately 1100–539 B.C.

7. **Babylon:** ancient city which was the capital of Babylonia, an ancient empire in southwest Asia in what is now southern Iraq. It flourished between 2100 and 689 B.C.

8. **shaman's:** belonging to a priest or medicine man of shamanism (shamanism is the religion of certain peoples of northeast Asia, based on a belief in good and evil spirits who can be influenced only by the shamans).

secret to accumulate knowledge and to establish the truth. Until Dianetics these commodities have been owned by philosophy of either the esoteric[9] or the monotony schools or had been used by the charlatan[10]—with or without surplice[11]—to lure and ensnare.

Dianetics moved into a dark age of reason where only a physical universe fact was given credence. When Dianetics was born every free thinker man had known had long since been burned or poisoned or dust-binned[12] into the curriculums of "universities." It was an age where renown awaited only the manufacturer—not the inventor—of the new can opener, where sanity was adjusted with electrodes and philosophy was made with Univacs.[13] *Knowledge* and the *secret* being the total assets of vested interest,[14] Dianetics was hit with violence from many quarters. Medicine, entirely cognizant that it could not cure nor even alleviate the majority of man's ills, yet, like a prima donna[15] who can but croak yet resists the incoming next act, bluntly and viciously condemned in leading weekly magazines any further glance toward knowledge and truth. The government, fighting a war at the time, entirely cognizant that its pilot supply was old and slow, yet could not communicate on any subject which might remedy the matter. The Better Business Bureaus of the U.S., an organization solidly behind anything good and solid,

---

9. **esoteric:** intended only for people with special knowledge or interest.

10. **charlatan:** a person who pretends to have expert knowledge or skill that he doesn't have; a fake.

11. **surplice:** a loose, white, wide-sleeved outer garment worn by the clergy and choir of some churches.

12. **dust-binned:** ash-canned; garbage-canned.

13. **Univacs:** *Trademark* electronic computing devices. [from Univ(ersal) A(utomatic) C(omputer)].

14. **vested interest:** the person or group, etc., who benefits the most from existing business or financial systems.

15. **prima donna:** the principal woman singer in an opera or concert.

---

upheld the objection of capital[16] to this new idea; the Communist Party, being solidly against any alteration of the mind since that would undoubtedly alter devotion, went to considerable lengths to assist the stand of capital. To anyone who wanted a monopoly on knowledge and truth Dianetics was an enemy. To them it was a degraded, wicked, fraudulent hoax—or so they said. However, there happens to be a principle that anything which is thoroughly understood ceases. Their opinion of Dianetics could not have been correct because Dianetics is still here.

During the ensuing four years of commotion, much happened. The only orderly and progressive thing which happened was that Dianetics went on encroaching into the territory of the *secret* along the roadway of *knowledge* to discover nearer *truth*.

The primary assault of Dianetics was upon reverence and forms. The first book was written as a javelin directed into the doubtlessly sacrosanct[17] vitals[18] of philosophical departments and literature. It was carefully careless with its commas in the belief that commas, contrary to the prevailing mode, have little power to disturb an ultimate truth. The first book was written to be read and understood, and it was written to upset and override and warn off those who would give it the fate of being reverable.[19] And the first book was written to be used by anyone who could understand it—and the way it was written, this of course could not include the extant mental charlatan (spelled "psychiatrist") nor the professional dabbler in abilities—the psychologist. As one had learned these two could not be trained and if they could have been, wouldn't have been interested in the

---

16. **capital:** owners of wealth used in business collectively: distinguished from labor.

17. **sacrosanct:** above or beyond change, criticism or interference.

18. **vitals:** the essential parts of something.

19. **reverable:** worthy of being regarded with deep respect, love and awe.

---

proposed goals, it was necessary that a new breed of feline come into being—the auditor[20]—and the auditor did.

Now this adventure along the road of knowledge toward truth was very shiny new in 1950. It was not quite so new but much shinier in 1954. Certain promises were made in 1950 in the last chapter of *Dianetics: The Modern Science of Mental Health*. And these promises have now been kept.

Man *can* be cleared.[21] He can be cleared—brought to the condition described in Chapter Two of the first book—by a well-studied and competent auditor in a relatively short length of time.

This book contains the processes by which clearing can be accomplished. This does not mean that auditors do not have to be trained—for we have found that they do. It does mean that an auditor who has been trained and processed can now take these newer processes and run them as directed and can achieve the result of Clear.

Thus, in *Dianetics 55!* we have, actually, the *Second Book* of Dianetics. Everyone has assigned the title First Book to *Dianetics: The Modern Science of Mental Health*. But nobody has ever referred to *Science of Survival*, published in 1951, as the Second Book. They haven't because it obviously wasn't. *Science of Survival* was a first book in its own right. It was the first book of and

20. **auditor:** a person trained and qualified in applying Dianetics and/or Scientology processes and procedures to individuals for their betterment; called an *auditor* because auditor means "one who listens."

21. **cleared:** brought to the state of Clear. The name of a state achieved through auditing or an individual who has achieved this state. A Clear is a being who no longer has his own reactive mind. A Clear is an unaberrated person and is rational in that he forms the best possible solutions he can on the data he has and from his viewpoint. The Clear has no engrams which can be restimulated to throw out the correctness of computation by entering hidden and false data.

under Plan C in the last chapter of the real first book. *Science of Survival* adventured into causation, not into the resolution of problems outlined in the First Book.

Thus, there has never been a second book of Dianetics. Such a book would have to take the exact problems of the first book, and, in the terms and reference of the first book, resolve these problems.

Well, as one looks over fiction novels and technical volumes in general he finds that a four-year—almost five—lag between an author's first and second volume would discover his public to have waned. But when we take up a subject of the status of Dianetics, and when we realize that it is condensing into a few years some thousands of years of doing, we see that a lag of four or five years between volumes isn't so very bad.

What happened in those four or five years? Many things. Somehow, for one thing, research and development was financed and the basic organization, after many limpings, survived. A lot of petty things happened which in another decade will be bone dust—for none of these things, none of the tales of terror, the attacks, the financing, the business advances, were permitted to interrupt the only thing that *can* mean any difference—the product of years of steady gain on the road of knowledge toward the goal of ultimate truth.

Knowledge, truth, secrets—they are the guts and anatomy of life. They must not then be owned. They must not then be hidden or bent. They must be permitted to stand out in the bold sunlight for all to see, for only when they are to be seen are they safe things to have, to hold, to know.

This is the Second Book of Dianetics. It *could* mean a new Earth, it could mean a new freedom. But whatever it means it cannot mean *nothing* in the sense man uses that word—for you cannot unveil the *secret* and have it ever be quite so secret ever again.

L. Ron Hubbard
Phoenix, 1954

1

Dianetics

1

Dianetics

Why should anyone want to know anything about the human mind? And for that matter, why should anyone believe that knowledge of the human mind is either unobtainable or undesirable? Why should men ostensibly[1] seeking answers to the mind stray so far from it as to examine rats and entirely avoid looking at human beings? And why should anyone pretending to treat the mind stray so far afield as electric shock?

The answers are relatively simple. Anyone who knows the structure, function and dynamics of the human mind is very difficult to control. The only way a mind can be controlled is by enforcing upon it ignorance of itself. As far as study and treatment is concerned, a mind which has been made ignorant of itself would have to have restored to it awareness of its fundamentals before it could be considered to be recovered. And when one restores full awareness to a mind one is no longer able to victimize it; and the profession or society would have to move out of slave orientation into action by freedom and consent, were it to be effective.

Just as you do not want people to control you, so you

---

1. **ostensibly:** apparently; seemingly.

should want knowledge of yourself and others. Just as you fight away from knowingness concerning self, so you will be controlled.

A simple and conclusive science of mind is a vital necessity in any society which desires to become free and remain free. The only elements in a society which would combat or contest or dispute an effort to attain such a science would be those interests which desired, by ignorance, to maintain their control of a slavery. Each and every impulse of freedom is an impulse toward sanity, toward health, toward happiness. Every impulse toward slavery is an impulse in the direction of misery, disease and death. One can say alike of the arthritic and the neurotic that the basic cause of disturbance, physical or mental, germinated[2] in efforts to reduce the freedom of the individual, the group or mankind.

Dianetics is an effort toward the attainment by man of a level of freedom where decency and happiness can prevail, and where knowledge of the mind itself would prevent the unscrupulous use of the mechanisms of slavery. Dianetics can be contested, it can be vilified, its founder and practitioners can be publicly pilloried,[3] but Dianetics cannot be ignored. It could neither be drowned in praise, nor burned in some purge to its total eradication, for it is a wonderfully observable fact that the one impulse in man which cannot be erased is his impulse toward freedom, his impulse toward sanity, toward higher levels of attainment in all of his endeavors. This is man's one saving grace.[4] And because Dianetics is such an impulse, and because its basic purposes, from the moment of its conception, have been

---

2. **germinated:** started developing or growing.

3. **pilloried:** exposed to ridicule, public contempt, scorn or abuse.

4. **saving grace:** quality that makes up for other generally negative characteristics.

dedicated unswervably[5] to the attainment of even greater freedom it cannot perish—a fact which will become doubtlessly more annoying to the slave masters as the years roll on.

There is much argument upon which we could adventure concerning whether Dianetics is an art or a science, whether it is a humanity or a hoax, but all this would avail us very little for we would only be quibbling with words. Dianetics is what it is, and the totality of it can best be summed by the description, "an understanding of man." We do not care whether or not it is a science. We do not care whether or not it is more properly cataloged under adventure or mystery. We do care whether or not it is promulgated and known, for everywhere it walks slavery ceases. That mind which understands itself is the mind of a free man. It is no longer prone to obsessive behavior, unthinking compliances, covert innuendoes.[6] It is at home in an environment, not a stranger. It is the solver of problems and the maker of games. A mind that is enslaved is weak. A mind that is free is powerful, and all the power there is, is defined by and contained in freedom.

Why should you know something about your mind? A question of a similar magnitude would be "Why should you live?" A science fiction writer once conceived a world composed entirely of machines, composed to a point where the machines were repaired by other machines, which in turn were repaired by yet other machines, and so the circle went 'round and the machines survived. He wrote this story from the fondest belief of nuclear physicists[7] that there is only a machine, that man derived

5. **unswervably:** in a manner not turning aside in movement or direction; not deviating from the straight or direct course.

6. **innuendoes:** indirect remarks, gestures or references usually implying something derogatory.

7. **nuclear physicists:** scientists in that branch of physics which deals with atoms, their nuclear structure and the behavior of nuclear particles.

from some spontaneous combustion of mud, that the soul does not exist, that freedom is impossible, that all behavior is stimulus-response,[8] that causative thought cannot exist. What a world this would be! And yet this world, this pattern, is the goal of the slave makers. If every man could be depressed from his freedom to a point where he believed himself but a cog in an enormous machine, then all things would be enslaved. But who would there be to enjoy them? Who would there be to profit? Not the slave maker, for he is the first to succumb. He succumbs to his own mechanisms. He receives the full jolt of his own endeavors to entrap. What would be the purpose of this world of machines? There can be no purpose worth contemplating which does not include happiness and experience. When a man is no longer able to envision happiness as a part of his future, that man is dead. He has become nothing but an animated robot, without understanding, without humanity, perfectly willing, then, to compose missiles of such detonative[9] quality that an entire civilization could perish, and that the happiness of all could be destroyed in the experience of radiation—an experience which might be considered digestible by an atomic pile,[10] but not by a human being. Thus, as we depart from the concepts of freedom, we depart into a darkness where the will, the fear, and the brutality, of one or a few, no matter how well educated, may yet obliterate everything for which we have worked, everything for which we have hoped. This is what happens when the machine runs wild, and when man, become a machine, runs wild. Man can only become a machine when he is no longer capable of understanding his own beingness and has lost his contact with it. Thus it is of enormous importance that we

8. **stimulus-response:** given a certain stimulus something will automatically give a certain response.

9. **detonative:** tending to explode violently and noisily.

10. **atomic pile:** an early name for a nuclear reactor (an apparatus in which a nuclear fission chain reaction can be initiated, sustained and controlled, for generating heat or producing useful radiation).

understand something about the mind, that we understand we are minds, that we are not machines, and it is of enormous importance that man attain at once to some higher level of freedom where the machine reaction of destruction may be controlled, and where man himself can enjoy some of the happiness to which he is entitled.

Dianetics: The Modern Science of Mental Health was written into a world where atomic fission[11] was yet in its early stages. *Dianetics 55!* is being written in a world where bombs exist of such fury that a continent could be laid waste. The recent declaration of the Secretary of War of the United States of America that such weapons exist, and are capable of being used, and his assumption that men exist with such insufficiency of humanity that they would use such weapons, tells us that it is time someone, somewhere, took a hand in this game. The intimacy of his promises cannot be escaped. You would think anyone a madman who essayed[12] to destroy every book in every library in the United States and Russia. You would think a man quite insane if he insisted upon the destruction of all of your personal possessions. You would know he was mad when he insisted that the only course for the future was the destruction of your body and any future race to remember it. Only a raving, drooling madman could contemplate the ending of all goals everywhere on Earth. And only an apathetic fool would stand by motionless before the inevitable destruction of his most intimate dreams, his fondest hopes, his possessions—even on down to the identification cards and money in his wallet. Such destruction permits no inheritance. It means an end of everything for which we have all hoped, for which we and our ancestors have

---

11. **fission:** atomic fission, the splitting of the nucleus of an atom accompanied by conversion of part of the mass into energy. This is the principle of the atomic bomb.

12. **essayed:** tried; attempted.

---

strived, and it is my belief that an individual who can contemplate this with equanimity[13] and without an impulse to act is so lost to the race and lost to himself, to his family, and to his friends, that he must personally believe there is no hope for anything, anywhere, at any time. Such depravity is difficult to envision. We know, definitely, that the wrong thing to do is nothing. Whatever any situation may develop, we always have that answer. It is wrong to do nothing. The only time anyone has ever gotten into serious trouble was when he decided he could do nothing about something.

This was the entering threshold toward death. When one *knew*, at last, that he was powerless in the face of all fates, or of any one particular fate, he was, to that degree, a slave of those fates. Thus, the wrong thing to do in this world, at this time, is nothing. No matter what fantastic or incredible plan we adventure upon, no matter how we put it forward, it would still be better than the abandonment of all plans and all action. It may be that we have better plans than fantastic plans. It may be that we, possessed of a knowledge of the mind and of man, can yet restrain this dreadful crime of oblivion from occurring.

Dianetics, then, is a weapon. It is a timely weapon. It is the only weapon of defense in existence which can confront with equanimity nuclear fission. Dianetics can fail only if it is not used, only if those who know about it do not use it to its fullest extent. Were you to take the technologies of Dianetics this day and, seeking out anyone even remotely connected with the responsibility for waging atomic war, apply these techniques to him, you would soon have the man into a sufficiently high strata of humanity that he would recognize some of his responsibility to the human race. Your task would be made hard, for all those

13. **equanimity:** the quality of remaining calm and undisturbed; evenness of mind or temper; composure.

who are connected with the waging of war with atomic fission are restrained by law from receiving any psychotherapy. If this seems incredible to you, you should realize that anyone in a top-secret or confidential classification in a government is not supposed to impart any information of his calling. And it is the fear of governments that some of this information might be imparted to someone practicing in the field of mental healing. Thus, if anyone connected with nuclear fission is discovered to be undergoing processing[14] of any kind, he would be immediately relieved of his post and his top-secret classification would be cancelled. But this is not a hopeless picture. Supposing one processed them all and had all their top-secret classifications cancelled, who would be left? Or supposing one pointed out this idiocy with sufficient conviction to those in charge of (but who are not responsible for) the destinies of man, and made it mandatory that the sanity of anyone connected with the creation or use of atomic fission be required to have a sanity passport. Only the insane will destroy. Remember that! Only the insane would bring about the end of Earth. One of these men, fumbling forward, uncomprehending, a mere machine, given processing begins to realize that he is not without responsibility for the safety of humanity. Only when he is a slave could he be forced to use such weapons against mankind. There is no argument on Earth of sufficient emergency or violence to require war, much less war by atomic fission with the consequence of the destruction of at least one continent and, within a few years, the destruction of the planet Earth.

Who would believe that anyone could wipe a continent clean of life without at once so polluting the atmosphere of Earth as to endanger or eradicate all further life forms on this planet?

---

14. **processing:** the application of Dianetics or Scientology processes to someone by a trained auditor. The exact definition of processing is: the action of asking a preclear a question (which he can understand and answer), getting an answer to that question and acknowledging him for that answer. Also called *auditing.*

What argument could there be amongst men which could occasion such a fate for Earth? There is no such argument amongst men. Such an argument could arise amongst machines which, consciencelessly, by pushed buttons, reach conclusions for which they have no responsibility.

There are many ways in which a higher state of security could be attained for Earth. None of these ways include violence or revolution. All of them include a greater freedom for mankind. Dianetics is the key technology necessary for the control of atomic fission. Remember that, and remember also that Dianetics is a precision science, that it works only when it is used as a precision science. For if you are to accomplish anything with it, whether the rescue of a relative from the pain of continued psychosomatic[15] illness, of a group, a nation or a world, it works exactly along the lines it is designed. It does not work with innovations. It is a precision science. It has a precision mission. It contains more answers than man has ever had before, and it contains enough answers to make man free—if it is used!

---

15. **psychosomatic:** *psycho* refers to mind and *somatic* refers to body; the term *psychosomatic* means the mind making the body ill or illnesses which have been created physically within the body by derangement of the mind.

2

The Fundamentals of Life

2

The Fundamentals of Life

Much more broadly covered in Scientology,[1] the fundamentals of life yet differ in no way for man.

The basic subdivision in life is between ability and mechanics. This could also be described as a subdivision of quality and quantity, but less accurately.

Where mechanics have ability, the ability is only apparent and has been endowed into the mechanics by life. It is all right to suppose that an electronic brain is capable of thought as long as one realizes that life itself must necessarily be present in order to give cause and quality, or direction, to such a brain. An electronic brain will sit all day and do nothing unless life starts the machine running. It will give millions of answers, but none of these, no matter how sharp, have any meaning until they are viewed by life. The machine is never anything more than a

---

1. **Scientology:** Scientology applied religious philosophy. It is the study and handling of the spirit in relationship to itself, universes and other life. Scientology means *scio*, knowing in the fullest sense of the word, and *logos*, study. In itself the word means literally "knowing how to know." Scientology is a "route," a way, rather than a dissertation or an assertive body of knowledge. Through its drills and studies one may find the truth for himself. The technology is therefore not expounded as something to believe, but something to *do*.

servomechanism[2] to life. Indeed, a machine cannot even exist in the absence of life.

By mechanics we mean any and all of the objects, motions or spaces which exist. Foremost of these, and foremost in any mechanical scheme, is space. Next is energy. Next is condensed or solidified energy, called matter. And finally, always present in any mechanical arrangement or mechanic, that relative change of position of particles or objects known as time. Thus we have space, energy, matter and time. Whether we are considering a body running on any energy, an automobile or a mountain, we are still dealing with what we call here mechanics. Mechanics are always quantitative. There is always just so much distance or so much mass or so many hours. The quality of space, energy, matter and time has value only when viewed, used or monitored by life, and, indeed, cannot exist in the absence of life. Correct or not, this is workable and is our primary assumption. We have a word for mechanics compounded from matter, energy, space and time which is MEST. By MEST we mean any or all arrangements of energy of whatever kind, whether in fluid or object form, in space or spaces. We do not conceive life to have an energy, and therefore, any energy, even if directly produced by life, can be found to be embraced under the quantitative term MEST.

Life itself has quality and ability. The products of quality and ability are mechanics. Ability is demonstrated by the handling of matter, energy, space and time. Quality means simply "valued" or "having a value." No values, that is to say opinions, exist in the absence of life. In the matter of such a thing as an automatic switch, we might consider that the switch is capable of making a decision whether to be off or on. However, we must remember that the original decision that a switch was to be

---

2. **servomechanism:** a mechanism which serves, services or aids something.

made, and that "off" and "on" could be accomplished and, indeed, the design of the switch itself depended entirely upon life quality.

In the field of mechanics we do not discover creativeness. We discover varying condition, varying arrangement, deterioration and destruction of one or another form, but we do not discover any alteration in quantity. Indeed, the entire science of physics is predicated[3] upon the assumption of "conservation of energy," which is to say that energy, itself, cannot be created or destroyed but can only alter its forms. To this we might add "conservation of space," "conservation of matter" and "conservation of time." None of these things are capable, in themselves, of altering. They are not capable of more than change of position or alteration of form. The physicist is very fond of demonstrating that the breaking of a vase does no more than alter the relative position of the particles and the form, and that the burning of a piece of coal does not change the basic particles of matter, since if you were to collect all the smoke, all the ash and the particles which radiated from the burning and weighed them you would have the same weight as before the coal was burned. In other words, the quantity of matter does not change and, as above, it does not create to itself or add to itself in any way.

Life, it has been adequately established, can, however, create. It can create particles and it can add to mass. The demonstration of this on a man is an easily accomplished thing and is quite conclusive. A process known as the Remedy of Havingness[4] is capable of altering the weight of a man upwards of twenty to

---

3. **predicated:** founded (a statement, action, etc.) or based (upon).

4. **Remedy of Havingness:** a process that has a preclear mock up a mass in front of him and shove it into his body, and mock up another mass in front of him and throw it away, over and over. When the process has been done thoroughly and completely, the preclear should be able to reject or accept, at his own discretion, anything in his environment as well as anything in his engram bank.

thirty-five pounds even though there is no change whatsoever in the diet or living habits of that person. In other words, the life which is in the body of the man, and which is actually the man, can, by a certain process, increase the amount of mass of this man. Another process known as Perfect Duplication[5] can reverse this, and, again without change of diet or the living habits of a man, decrease the amount of mass of a man without the complications of heat or waste products being present. Thus, forthrightly and directly, in the same frame of reference as that used by the physicist, it is easily demonstrated that life does create mass and can cause mass to disappear.

As long ago as fifty years, as represented by an article in the *Encyclopedia Britannica*, it was fairly well understood that the study of physics should have begun with an examination of the mind. This article, under the heading of time and space, states that as space and time are mental phenomena their proper delineation and study begins in the field of the mind. Nineteenth-century "mental sciences" were insufficiently schooled in science to comprehend this, and the physicist, unaware in general of such a fact, did not consider that his proper province was the mind. Thus a misunderstanding existed in the humanities and in the sciences where one was depending upon the other, and the result came about that neither knew his proper field of endeavor. By undertaking a study of the mind from the orientation of physics, and with the application of all the principles known in chemistry, physics and mathematics (items in which the nineteenth-century psychologist was entirely unfamiliar, and which the twentieth-century psychologist utterly disdains), it was only then possible to produce some comprehension of this thing we call life in this place we call the physical universe.

---

5. **Perfect Duplication:** a process by which a preclear is gotten to create a perfect duplicate of an object. A perfect duplicate is an additional creation of the object, its energy and space, in its own space, in its own time, using its own energy.

Thus, that thing which considers, that thing which has opinions, that thing which creates, that thing which monitors, that thing which has goals and desires, and which can experience, is life. What we call space, time, energy, matter, forms of any kind, are the byproducts of, and are monitored by, life. Energy, whether in the form of a mental image, a body, a tree or a rock, is alike the byproduct of life. There is no faintest difference, save only density and wavelength, between the space you behold around you with your physical eyes and the spaces and forms you see when you close them and behold a mental image. These things, alike, are energies, and obey the various laws of energy.

Here, then, we have a unit or a quality capable of bringing into being quantities such as spaces, energies, masses and time, capable of changing and controlling these masses and energies, capable of adding to them or subtracting from them.

There is a considerable dissertation in *Dianetics: The Modern Science of Mental Health* concerning the awareness of awareness unit.[6] When this subject was first under investigation it was established that all was not a machine. Somewhere, in tracing back the various lines, it was necessary to strike a cause point, either simply to assume that there was a cause point or to actually discover one. Two words were used in connection with this causative agent. One of them was *analytical mind*, and the other, much more properly, *the awareness of awareness unit*. The awareness of awareness unit, as its name implies, is aware of being aware, or aware of being alive. When one was looking at or discussing the analytical mind, one was aware of something else: that the awareness of awareness unit became connected in some fashion with computers, or analyzers, in order to handle and

---

[6] **awareness of awareness unit:** an actuality of no mass, no wavelength, no position in space or relation in time, but with the quality of creating or destroying mass or energy, of locating itself or creating space and in re-relating time.

control the remainder of the physical beingness. The term *analytical mind* then meant the awareness of awareness unit plus some evaluative circuit[7] or circuits, or machinery, to make the handling of the body possible.

The other item discussed broadly in *Dianetics: The Modern Science of Mental Health* was the reactive mind. This mind was a stimulus-response mind which depended upon exterior direction for its action and reaction. The reactive mind was conceived to be a collection of records, in picture form, so arranged as to make a complete pattern of experience, capable by its pattern alone of evaluating the conduct and behavior of the individual. The pictures contained in the reactive mind are now called "facsimiles," for they are no more and no less than pictures, like photographs, taken of the universe around the individual and retained by him. A specialized kind of facsimile was the "engram." This differed from other mental pictures because it contained, as part of its content, unconsciousness and physical pain. The definition of an engram is: a picture of "a moment of pain and unconsciousness." The reactive mind was conceived to have more of these engrams than the analyzer. But the analyzer was seen to have some of these, too, except they were a lighter form and were a lock[8] on the engram in the reactive memory bank. Indeed, when one considered the reactive mind he was actually considering what is, in the electronic brain, a memory bank. Instead of cards or a card-file system the reactive mind contained pictures. These pictures were filed and were drawn out of the files by the environment, which contained restimulators.[9] The

---

7. **circuit:** a division of your own mind that seems to make up another personality and this other personality affects you, argues with you and so forth.

8. **lock:** a mental image picture of a nonpainful but disturbing experience the person has had, which depends for its force on earlier secondaries and engrams which the experience has restimulated (stirred up).

9. **restimulators:** anything in the individual's surroundings which is sufficiently similar to something in his reactive mind that it causes part of his reactive mind to become restimulated.

presence of these pictures could alter form and could alter behavior. The eradication of one of these engrams by the early erasure[10] techniques of Dianetics was found to alter the stimulus-response behavior of the individual.

Here we were confronting three kinds of minds. One was the causative agent, the awareness of awareness unit, which did not appear to have any byproducts but which was impinged upon another mind called the analytical mind, which on a machine basis analyzed situations rationally, and was sane and rational, and a third kind of mind even further remote from the awareness of awareness unit, which acted without the consent of the causative agent and did not in any way consult it. Now on a very careful review of this we see that the analytical mind and the reactive mind, alike, are byproduct mechanical minds. Alike, they depend upon energy, spaces, storage and other quantitative things. The awareness of awareness unit, however, is itself decision, is itself knowingness. It delivers into the analytical mind and its systems various knowingnesses to be handled on a mechanical basis, and unwittingly delivers into the hands of the reactive mind—which is totally a mechanical thing—the right to alter and correct the analytical mind. Apparently, then, we have here a causative agent and two machines. We might as well, then, take the obvious conclusion that there is the awareness of awareness unit, and that this in some fashion handles machinery, and that the analytical mind, the reactive mind, and even the body and the environment, are mechanical. One item here is qualitative and decisional—the awareness of awareness unit. All other items are subordinate to it and depend for their conclusions either upon it or upon the environment. Here again we have quality versus quantity.

A further demonstration of this awareness of awareness unit

---

10. **erasure:** the action of erasing (rubbing out) locks, secondaries or engrams.

in action is quite convincing. A machine, a meter, which is built in every tradition of physics and electronics, and which is composed of nothing more or less than the usual meters and gauges and electrodes, can detect the production of energy by the analytical mind. This machine demonstrates conclusively that the awareness of awareness unit can predict and cause an energy reaction to occur at will. It goes further and demonstrates that the awareness of awareness unit can bring about, without further contact, an energy flow in a body at a distance. This is a very startling demonstration and is one of the more significant electrical discoveries of recent times. The conditions of the experiment are sufficiently rigorous[11] to dispel any doubt in the mind of a physicist concerning the authenticity of occurrence.

If there were no energy being created by the awareness of awareness unit, then one would be at a loss to account for mental energy pictures, for these things, being made at a tremendously rapid rate, have considerable mass in them—mass which is measurable on a thing as common and everyday as the bathroom scales.

As soon as it was discovered how facsimiles (these mental energy pictures) came into being it was also discovered that they were actual energy and not "an idea of energy" as they had been supposed to be in the past. The facsimile and the engram come into action by resistance. The awareness of awareness unit resists a scene in the physical universe, either resisting its approach or departure, and thus by this resistance makes a print. This print is made in a moving fashion, like a motion picture, and is complete in every detail. Later on the individual can call back this print and take a look at it, and will find it to have in it the exact forces which were in the original version in the physical universe. The awareness of awareness unit does this so easily

---

11. **rigorous:** rigidly precise; thoroughly accurate or exact.

that it has been completely unaware of what it was doing. Now, when the awareness of awareness unit makes a print, trying to restrain something from going away, or trying to restrain it from approaching, and considers that the survival of its body is being violated or threatened, it files this print in such a way that it will not have to look at it again. But this does not mean that an approximation of the print by the physical environment cannot reactivate the print independently. In other words, when the awareness of awareness unit puts away and does not want to look again at such a facsimile, the facsimile itself begins to have a power over the awareness of awareness unit. The collected files of these nonsurvival experiences come together and are the reactive mind. The awareness of awareness unit could be conscious of these, but chooses not to be. Thus the environment can restimulate this reactive mind and can cause changes of behavior and bodily form such as overweight, psychosomatic ills or even fixed expressions or gestures.

The essence of time is change. Where there is no change there is no time. Thus, something which is unchanging is enduring. If a thing has no change in it, it will then "float" in all time, since it does not assign itself to any changingness, being a thing of no change. Thus we discover that silences and no-motions "float" in time and we discover that every place on the time track where the awareness of awareness unit has taken a picture of silence, has resented or restrained silence, it then has an energy mass which will "float" or stay with it, whatever time it assigns to itself, and we get the composition of the physical universe. The physical universe is composed of "floating" or *forever* energy. If this did not work out in processing and if it were not a usable principle it would not be included in this text.

In view of the fact that these facsimiles, particularly those of silence, can "stay with" the individual, then we get the entire mechanism we call "restimulation" where the environment reactivates a facsimile, which then acts back against the body or awareness of awareness unit of the person. This is a very simple system of stimulus-response. We discover, then, that engrams, or facsimiles in general, have a tendency to hang up on all of their silent or motionless spots. Thus a facsimile may contain considerable action and yet be stuck at one point of no-motion. Here we have a no-motion on either side of which there is motion. The no-motion point hangs up and is not contacted by the awareness of awareness unit, since the awareness of awareness unit is looking, in general, for motion. Thus we get a phenomenon known as "stuck on the time track" where an individual can believe himself to be at some distant point in the past. The facsimile or engram in which he is "caught" has almost as much reality to him as a condition of existence as his present-time environment. When he becomes entirely psychotic, the facsimile or engram has far more reality to him than his present-time environment. Thus we have aberration and psychosomatic illness.

In early Dianetics, the way this condition was alleviated was by addressing the pictures themselves and persuading the awareness of awareness unit to erase them by recounting them and reexperiencing them. Because this took a long time, and because auditors had a tendency to abandon half-erased incidents, the technologies—while workable—were not conclusive. Thus, more research and investigation had to be entered upon in order to establish the best way to handle this situation.

3

The Awareness of Awareness Unit

3

The Awareness of Awareness Unit

In examining the individuality and identity of the individual, one discovers that the individual *is* himself, and not his byproducts. The individual is not his analytical mind, he is not his reactive mind, he is not his body any more than he is his house or his car. He might consider himself to be associated with his analytical mind, his reactive mind, his house, his body, his car, but he is not these things. He is himself. The individual, the personality, *is* the awareness of awareness unit, and the awareness of awareness unit is the person. As this awareness of awareness unit confuses itself further and further with the pictures it has made of its surroundings, it conceives itself more and more to be an object; until at last, when it has gone entirely down the Tone Scale[1] it has arrived at the point where its fondest belief is that it is an object.

Just as you would not say that John Jones was his car, so must you also say—when you perceive this clearly—that John Jones is not his analytical mind or his reactive mind, his body or his clothes. John Jones is an awareness of awareness unit, and all

---

1. **Tone Scale:** a scale which shows the emotional tones of a person. These, ranged from the highest to the lowest, are, in part, serenity, enthusiasm (as we proceed downward), conservatism, boredom, antagonism, anger, covert hostility, fear, grief, apathy.

there is of him that is capable of knowing and being aware is John Jones, an awareness of awareness unit.

When we have arrived at a state where John Jones himself knows that he is an awareness of awareness unit—it is not his analytical mind, his reactive mind, his body, his clothes, his house, his car, his wife or his grandparents—we have what is called in Dianetics, a Clear. A Clear is simply an awareness of awareness unit which knows it is an awareness of awareness unit, can create energy at will, and can handle and control, erase or recreate an analytical mind or a reactive mind.

The difference of approach is this: Instead of erasing all the things with which the awareness of awareness unit is in conflict, we make the awareness of awareness unit capable of besting and controlling all those things with which he thought he had to be in conflict. In other words, we raise the determinism of an individual up to a point where he is capable of controlling his mental pictures and the various byproducts of life. When he is capable, so far as his ability is concerned, of controlling and determining the action of these things, he is no longer aberrated. He can recall anything he wants to recall without the aid and assistance of energy masses. He can be what he wants to be. He has had restored to himself a considerable freedom.

About the only difficulty we have in accomplishing this state of Clear, with all the power and ability appended thereto, is the fact that individuals come to believe that they have to have certain things in order to go on surviving. Actually, an awareness of awareness unit cannot do anything else but survive. He is unkillable. Yet his byproducts are destroyable, and, confusing himself with his byproducts, he begins to believe that he has to have or do certain things in order to survive. His anxiety becomes so great on this that he will even believe that he has to have problems in order to survive. An awareness of awareness unit is very unhappy unless it has some mass or space of some kind and does not have various problems to solve.

For a very long time in Dianetics we looked far for the "One-Shot Clear."[2] Such a thing has come into existence and is workable on over fifty percent of the current populace of mankind. The One-Shot Clear depends, of course, on getting the awareness of awareness unit at a distance from and in control of its various byproducts so that it no longer confuses itself with its byproducts. The astonishing speed with which fifty percent of the human race can be cleared is believable only when you put it into action. The magic words are "Be three feet back of your head." This is the One-Shot Clear. If the existence of a One-Shot Clear or a process is indigestible to people, it is because they have so long contemplated objects and have their attention so thoroughly fixed upon objects that they can no longer view space. And the idea of viewing space, the idea of being without objects, is so antipathetic to them that they feel they must condemn any effort which might take from them the proximity of some of their fondest possessions.

It is so strongly antipathetic to man to look at space that one of the basic processes of Dianetics—causing him to look at spots in space—will cause a rather low-toned individual to become quite violently ill at his stomach. The nausea resulting simply from contemplating empty space is discoverable only in those who have a great deal of trouble with possessions and who are unable to have things. From having to have things they have gotten to a point where they do not believe they can have anything anymore. Thus, being asked to contemplate an emptiness of any kind is enough to cause a violent physical reaction.

2. **One-Shot Clear:** the one phrase or one action given once, or repeated, which would bring into being the Clear as described in *Dianetics: The Modern Science of Mental Health.*

Hence, this whole subject of "Clear" and exteriorization, as it is technically termed, is very antipathetic to the remaining fifty percent of the human race who cannot be hit instantly with this one-shot button.

Fifty percent of the people you walk up to, if you do not preselect your preclears—a person on the road to being Clear—will immediately exteriorize, be a distance from their body, and behold themselves as capable of handling a great many things they before considered impossible to control, the moment you say "Be three feet back of your head." The remaining fifty percent will look at you with varying puzzlement. These know they are a body. These know they are an object, and these know (most of them) that they would get sick at their stomachs if they contemplated being all by themselves in space. They would believe that it would be impossible to control a body while being three feet behind it. Thus, one gets into an immediate argument with such people, and they wish to go into the various deeper significances. If these people were lost to us with current Dianetic processes, we would still have gained many percentile over any past effort to do something for the race or about the mind.

In the past, even when we look as short a time ago as 1949, we discover that man in general did not possess the ability to get a recovery percentage in patients higher than twenty-two percent. Oddly enough, whether it was a witch doctor at work, a psychoanalyst, a psychiatrist, a psychologist, a medical doctor or any other practitioner, simple assurance and a pat on the back yet brought about twenty-two percent cured. This fact, not looked at very carefully by practitioners, caused people to believe that the only thing that was wrong with the mind was that people thought something was wrong with the mind and all anybody needed was a cheering word and it would all be all right. Twenty-two percent of any population will recover if anything is done for them. The remaining seventy-eight percent are not quite so lucky. When we can raise the percentage even to thirty percent we are doing more than has ever been done before. When any practice gets less than twenty-two percent recovery, then that practice is actually definitely harming people, for if all the practitioner did was be at home in his office and give cheery reassurance to his patients he would get this twenty-two percent. He would have to be very active and depressive in order to decrease this amount of "cures." Now, when we suddenly vault to the figure of fifty percent we know we are closing with the answer. Thus, we could relax at this very point, confident that we have done more in the field of healing than has ever before been done.

However, it is not good enough within our framework. In the first place, if we wish to treat people involved with the government, people involved with ruling, people involved with the material sciences — such as physicists and chemists — we are dealing with almost entirely the remaining "resistive" fifty percent. This does not mean that a person, simply by exteriorizing, is weaker. It means that a person with continuous contact with the physical universe and continuous harassment and concern over the state of objects or energy is apt to get what we call "interiorized."[3]

A recent series of cases undertaken to demonstrate how far we had to go and what we had to do in order to bring results in this remaining fifty percent has now concluded successfully. With modern techniques, very, very closely followed, auditors trained by Scientology organizations have been successfully clearing cases which were resistive and did not improve on all earlier processes as of 1951, '52, '53 and the bulk of '54. The certainty of clearing the first fifty percent simply with the magic

---

3. **interiorized:** having gone into something too fixedly and become part of it too fixedly.

words has been followed now with a certainty of handling the remaining fifty percent. This presents a rather different scene and attitude than in 1950 where an auditor had to be "intuitive" and had to work endlessly, it seemed, to produce gains on cases, much less clearing. My own percentages in clearing people do not count, and I learned early (with some puzzlement) that what I did with a preclear and the results I obtained with a preclear were not the results which would be obtained by another auditor. It was this fact alone which caused research and investigation to be continued at such lengths, and for processes to be codified so closely. For first we had to know the processes, and then we had to know how to train auditors, and finally we are obtaining these clearing results.

Any Clear earlier obtained was known to be Clear simply by the fact that he could recall at will by pictures, or could perform certain other feats. Actually, a person was only able to stay Clear, when he was not immediately involved with either his analytical or his reactive mind. And those Clears which remained stable had been put unwittingly into a much more advanced state than had been supposed, even by the auditor. It was an investigation of these Clears which led forward into the techniques we have now. It was found that many of them were simply wide-open cases which had become rather able to read their own facsimiles. Several had simply increased their abilities to a point so senior to other people's ability that everyone agreed they should be called "Clear." And then there was the actual Clear. The actual Clear, on close questioning, even though he himself had not always noticed it, conceived himself now to be some distance from the body. Those Clears which remained stable and continued to perform and function despite the convulsions of life were these who had been stably exteriorized. This may be a datum which is very hard for some Dianeticists to assimilate, but again the difficulty would stem only from the fact that these would be unwilling to look at space or would be afraid of being disenfranchised.[4] Such people are very frightened of losing their bodies. But this is a fact with which we cannot argue: that so far as psychosomatic illness is concerned, it is best resolved by exteriorization. One has the individual step back from his body, look at it, and patch it up, and that is about all there is to psychosomatic illness. There is, of course, an electronic structure of the body which one can direct the person's attention to, but I have seen the shape of a face change in moments, I have seen psychosomatic illnesses disappear in seconds, and as long as there was any physical structure left to work with at all I have seen the problem of psychosomatic illness pushed so far in the background, as a problem, that we no longer think in these terms, and indeed do not consider Dianetics well used when it is only addressed to psychosomatic illness and aberration.

Our emphasis today is upon ability. We have found that the more we increase the ability of a person the better the byproducts around him become. Simply by increasing an individual's ability to walk or talk we can change his physical beingness and his mental outlook.

By this theory it would be enough to have somebody learn how to make pottery, or drive a car, or sing, or speak in public to increase his mental and physical health. And indeed, on investigation we discover that these things are therapeutic, but we discover that they are limited in their therapy because the talents which an individual learns in this fashion are talents involved entirely with the handling and orientation of the body, and he is not being entirely influenced merely by his body. He is being influenced as well by the computing machinery which he calls his analytical mind and by the more insidious[5] and less obvious

---

4. **disenfranchised:** deprived of a privilege, right or power.

5. **insidious:** operating in a slow or not easily apparent manner; more dangerous than seems evident.

machinery called his reactive mind. Furthermore, by these increases in ability he is not brought up to a point where he can control or handle his entire environment. Such an ability can be developed only by, and in, the awareness of awareness unit itself. When it is learning to do something via the body it is not learning to do something directly, it is learning to do something with help—the help of arms and legs, face, voice, eyes; and thus hobby therapy is limited even though it is quite positive.

Looking a little further along this line one discovers that the awareness of awareness unit has peculiar abilities. First and foremost of its abilities is to be where it likes to be and look. It does not need eyes. It does not need a vehicle in which to travel. All it needs to do is to postulate its existence in a certain location and then look from that point of existence. In order to do this it has to be willing to be cause. It has to be willing to be an effect. But if it can do this it can go much further—it can create and change space. Furthermore, it can erase at a glance facsimiles and engrams.

Now when we get into such capabilities people are liable to believe that we have entered the field of mysticism[6] or spiritualism.[7] But an inspection of these fields demonstrates the people in them not to be very able. Mysticism and other such practices are reverse practices. Rather than controlling the reactive bank, the analytical mind, the body, the environment, they seek, very markedly, to withdraw from the necessity to control. This is downward ability, and while I might be accused of maligning these fields, I can only look at the people I have known in these fields and at the fact that I myself studied in

---

6. **mysticism:** a doctrine of an immediate spiritual intuition of truths believed to transcend ordinary understanding, or of a direct, intimate union of the soul with God through contemplation or ecstasy.

7. **spiritualism:** the belief that the dead survive as spirits which can communicate with the living, especially with the help of a third party.

these fields in the East and know their limitations. People are apt to confuse exteriorization with astral walking. As you sit there reading this book you are definitely and positively aware of sitting there, and of this book. There is no question about whether or not you are looking at a book. You don't believe yourself to be projected, and you don't have to guess where you are, and you don't think you have to create some sort of image in order to look at anything. You are simply sitting there reading a book. This is exteriorization. If you were cleared, and, with your body at home, you were in a library, you could read in the library just as well, with the limitation that you might not have a good grasp on pages. You would certainly know you were in the library. There would be no question about this. There would be no question about the text on the periodicals on the table. There would be no question about the quality and personality of the librarian and other people sitting there. Being Clear does not enter into it, guesswork. You would not be concerned with telepathy, with reading people's minds, and with other such bric-a-brac. You would simply know what you wanted to know. Further, you wouldn't have to use a system for finding out what you know. You would simply know it.

If man cannot face what he is, then man cannot be free. For, an awareness of awareness unit surrounded entirely by energy masses, and believing that it itself is completely these masses, is in a difficult and desperate state. It believes, for instance, that in order to go from one address to another it has to take the energy mass along with it. This is not true. One might carry a body around in order to speed up one's conversation, in order to have a problem, in order to get some attention and interest from people, but one would not carry a body around because one had to have a body.

The general attitude of a person who is cleared is the most interesting thing to observe. Only a cleared person has a very definite tolerance for the behavior of others. People before they are cleared are in a varying degree of distrust of other people. They are hiding, or protecting, or owning things to such a degree that they do not dare separate themselves from them.

There is a certain fear of an exteriorized person. There is a belief that he might do them wrong. Actually, one is done wrong by the weaklings of this world, not the strong men. One does not have to enslave and control by force those whose conduct he does not fear. When you find an individual who is bent entirely upon a course of the arduous control of the motions of others, you are looking at an individual who is afraid. By their fear you shall know them.

Another slight difficulty in the state of exteriorization is that one has a tendency to let things be more or less as they are. Up to a certain point one is content to let the game run and take part in it and have fun with it. The point, of course, is the destruction of the playing field. Life, to a Clear, is no more and no less than a game, and the only thing which he would consider somewhat unpardonable in behavior would be the wiping out of such a playing field. But if he were even higher in such a state he could, theoretically, make his own playing field. However, if he did this he would find difficulty getting into communication with other live beings, unless, of course, he made them, which is a rather unsatisfactory state of affairs since one never quite forgets that he did so.

Moral conduct is conduct by a code of arbitrary laws. Ethical conduct is conduct out of one's own sense of justice and honesty. When you enforce a moral code upon people you depart considerably from anything like ethics. People obey a moral code because they are afraid. People are ethical only when they are strong. One could say that the criminals of earth are those upon whom moral codes have been too forcefully enforced. As an example of this take the cliché object, the minister's son. Ethical conduct does not mean promiscuous, abandoned or lawless conduct. It means conduct undertaken and followed because one has a sense of ethics, a sense of justice and a sense of tolerance. This is self-determined morality. A Clear has this to a very marked degree. By actual check of many such cases, their moral behavior is intensely superior to that of people who pride themselves on "being good." The point arises because law and order depends for its existence upon its necessity in the field of morals, and it looks with a sort of horror on somebody who would be good without recourse to, or threat from, the forces of law and order. Such a person would be rather hard to have around. He would cut down the number on the police force quite markedly.

The state of Clear, then, is obtainable and is desirable, and now that we can accomplish it with greater positiveness than in 1950 is found to be superior to that described in the second chapter of *Dianetics: The Modern Science of Mental Health*.

The way one goes about being Clear, or creating a Clear, is simple, but requires a certain code of conduct called the Auditor's Code, and requires, we have discovered, a considerable amount of training. Clearing another person is a highly specialized ability. This ability must be raised in individuals before they can easily and successfully undertake such a project. Witnessing this is the fact that while many of the processes involved in clearing have been available for a very, very long time, very few people have successfully used them. The discovery of why this was, was quite as important as the state of Clear itself. The remedy of this disability lies in training and processing. The activity of creating a Clear is known as "processing" and is undertaken by one individual on behalf of another individual. "Self-clearing" has not been found possible where the individual was badly mired in his own case.

Enormously subordinate to the goal of Clear, but enormously senior to man's various healing activities in the mind, spirit and body, the very processes which lead up to Clear remedy, whether one wants them to or not, a great many of the ills of the individual. One can take one of these modern processes and run it all by itself, and accomplish more with Dianetics than man had previously accomplished in the field of healing. When one has the answers, of course, applying those answers to minor psychosomatic difficulties, or aberrations, or spiritual unrest is elementary. But again we have discovered that there is no real substitute for training either at the hands of an already trained and skilled auditor or, best, from a central organization.[8]

The awareness of awareness unit was not readily discoverable in the field of physics because physics is entirely concerned with mechanics. Physics starts with the assumption of the conservation of energy, the existence of space, and goes on into further complexity from there. The awareness of awareness unit is one step earlier than all this, and its existence was unsuspected by a misdefinition in the field of physics. That was the definition of a static. A static, in physics, is called something which is "in an equilibrium of forces." This object at rest in an equilibrium of forces is an interesting semantic puzzle. If we put a glass upon the table and then say that it is a static, we are telling a very bad lie. It is not in an equilibrium of forces. That glass happens to be travelling at 1,000 miles an hour just by reason of the fact that Earth is turning. It has seven other directions and speeds by reason of being part of the planet Earth, the solar system, and this galaxy. It cannot, then, be considered at rest. Thus no object can be considered at rest unless one considers something relatively at rest. The glass is at rest in relationship to the table, but this is not the physical definition.

---

8. **central organization:** a Scientology service organization.

The definition of a static disclosed something else of interest. There was a missing definition in the field of mathematics, and that was the definition of zero. The mathematician for ages has been using in all of his formulas a wild variable without suspecting it was there. He did not really encounter it until he got into the higher fields of nuclear physics. At this time, he encountered it so forcefully and knew it so little that he had to alter most of his mathematical conceptions in order to work with nuclear physics at all.

This wild variable was no less than zero. Zero, put down as a goose egg in a mathematical formula, would introduce many interesting variables. In the first place an absolute zero has never been obtained in this universe. It has only been approached. That is in terms of temperature. That is in terms of nonexistence. We can say there is a zero of apples, but that is still a qualified zero. We can say there were no apples, but that is further qualified as being in the past and is a past zero. We could say there will be no apples, and again we will have a zero qualified as being in the future. Zero was an absence of a thing, and this immediately violated the definition of zero as being no thing. The absoluteness of *no thing* had to be examined while we were examining the field of the mind and actually led to some very astonishing discoveries with regard to life itself and immediately pinpointed the existence of the awareness of awareness unit.

The proper and correct definition of zero would be "something which had no mass, which had no wavelength, which had no location in space, which had no position or relationship in time." This would be a zero. One could state it more shortly, if a little less correctly as "something without mass, meaning, or mobility."

It would be almost impossible to detach a dyed-in-the-wool[9]

---

9. **dyed-in-the-wool:** thoroughgoing; unchanging.

physicist from the concept that everything was a "something-ness" and that there was actually a "nothingness." However, there is a nothingness which has quality. It has potential, it has ability. It has the ability to perceive, it has the ability to create, the ability to understand, and the ability to appear and disappear, to its own satisfaction, in various positions in space. Furthermore, this thing could, we have demonstrated conclusively, manufacture or cause to vanish space, energy and masses, and could, quite additionally, reposition time.

These new concepts are actually advances in the field of physics and mathematics, and from the viewpoint of the physicist and the mathematician would only incidentally apply to the mind.

From this data we get the basic definition of a static, which is "an actuality of no mass, no wavelength, no position in space or relation in time, but with the quality of creating or destroying mass or energy, of locating itself or creating space, and in re-relating time." And thus we have the definition of an awareness of awareness unit. It is the definition of a static. It does not have quantity, it has quality. It does not have mechanics, it can produce mechanics, and it does have ability.

The foremost ability of the awareness of awareness unit is to have an idea, and to continue that idea, and to perceive the idea and its continuance in the form of mass, energy, objects and time. In the field of Scientology the fact that this awareness of awareness unit can also control or even make physical bodies is almost incidental. That is only a specialized branch of the game. In Dianetics this is a very important function, for one in Dianetics is working with man.

A static could also be called an orientation point. It would be from that point that it made and directed space, energy and objects. It would be from that point that it assigned meanings, and thus we have an essential difference between the awareness of awareness unit and its byproducts. These byproducts we can categorize as symbols. When we say "mechanics" we actually mean to some degree "symbols." A symbol is something that has mass, meaning and mobility—three M's. That is the technical definition of a symbol. An orientation point is something that controls symbols. The difference in ability of an awareness of awareness unit is how much it is an orientation point in relationship to how much it believes itself to be a symbol, or to have mass, meaning or mobility. Reduction from the state of awareness is into the condition of the symbol—mass, meaning and mobility. To get a clearer idea of this, you see the word *a* on this page. That has mass, even if very slight mass. It has meaning, since it conveys an idea when glanced at, and it certainly has mobility, since you can move the book around. Now you, looking at this book, have the role of an orientation point to the degree that you do not conceive yourself to have a fixed identity, a fixed position, a fixed mass. If you, looking at this book, have no real mass, if your name is not a tremendously fixed idea with you, and if you know you can move your body around without having to move with it, then you would very clearly and decisively be an orientation point. But if you think you have mass and are mass, and if you think you are your name, and if you think you have to move around only by moving the body around, then of course somebody else, something else, can be your orientation point. It may be your mother. It may be your home town or, if you are a mystic, it might even be some spirit. You would think of yourself as a symbol. Similarly, a symbol does not remember anything more than it symbolizes, and thus your memory to a large degree might be the memory of past allies—people who took care of you and to whom you were attached affectionately—and if you were in a lecture you would probably take notes rather than remember what was being said. An orientation point has the power of memory without record.

A symbol has the power of memory only to the degree that it *is* a record.

Thus we see that it is desirable that an individual does not identify himself with masses, but that he retain his ability to handle masses and objects and energy, to remember at will, without the need of records such as those in the reactive bank, or facsimile machines such as those in the analytical mind bank.

In any good, thorough investigation, one investigates to see what he will discover and to find better ways to do things. In any reliable investigation report one tells what he discovered and reports its character and nature. In this science we are doing just that. When we talk of the awareness of awareness unit we are not talking to be pleasing, to win friends or influence professors, we are simply telling you what has been discovered after twenty-five years of research and investigation in the field of the mind, having taken off from the platform[10] of physics and mathematics rather than philosophy. The awareness of awareness unit is a fact. It is a demonstrable fact, and the best way to demonstrate it is to use the processes which accomplish it, and then discover that the individual is more well, has a better memory, is better oriented, is more capable, is more ethical, is happier, has better command of time, can communicate better, is more willing to have friends, is less antisocial than the average person, and has a greater zest for living and getting things done. All these things can be accomplished by test.

In 1950 we often had occasion to demonstrate the existence of the engram. It seemed to be highly in question among those people who were extremely specialized—it said on their diplomas—in the field of the mind. To be accomplished in the field of the mind and yet not know anything about engrams or

---

10. **platform:** a statement of principles and policies.

facsimiles would be an idiotic state indeed, because the mind is composed of facsimiles and engrams, if one wishes to examine items or energy products. Well, as now, we were only interested in results. What can we *do* with this technology? If we can demonstrate with this technology that we can better the lives, tolerances, abilities of those around us, then certainly we will have done something. We have no place for philosophical arguments concerning this material. It is simply workable material. You do not argue with the directions on how to open a vacuum-packed can. If you don't follow them you don't get the can open. Or, not following them, and still being insistent upon it, you smash the can and ruin the contents. One would not go into a philosophic dissertation about the directions of opening a can. Obviously they are written by somebody who knows how to open cans, and any hours spent on getting this person to demonstrate that he really could open cans would be wasted time. The thing to do is simply to read the directions, follow them very closely, and see whether or not the can is opened. Although this seems to be a rather common sort of an example to apply to that noble creature, man, it is nevertheless the bluntest statement that could be made about the status of Dianetics and Scientology and their uses and purposes.

Dianetics has as its goal the repairing and patching up of this thing called, by the uninitiated, a civilization, taking its destiny out of the hands of madmen who think that the entire organism is simply a machine, and putting it in the hands of the same people, only this time with the ingredient of sanity added. There isn't even any point in trying to categorize Dianetics or say that it compares to psychology or mathematics or engineering, or any other activity, because it is obviously senior to all these activities and doesn't have to take any of these activities into account to work. All Dianetics needs to work is a trained auditor, a preclear and a little time in which to accomplish its processes. If these ingredients—the auditor, the preclear, and a little time—

were not available, then there would be no purpose in having any Dianetics at all, since there wouldn't be any human race.

The spirit in which these conclusions are advanced is intensely practical, and now that some nitwits, who probably don't get along with their wives and hate dogs, but who have worked themselves into the position of being able to, can knock a couple of atoms together, either by orders or by actual skill, and so tear up a very nice playing field, the presence of Dianetics in this world is not simply a practicality, but an urgency.

4

Accent on Ability

4

Accent on Ability

Almost anyone realizes that he can be better than he is, that he can do things better than he has been doing them. It is an entirely different thing to ask someone to realize that he is ill, aberrated or stupid. Why is it that a man can understand that he can be more capable and very often cannot understand that he is incapable? It would seem to follow that if a man realized he could be more capable, then he would realize at once that he was, to some degree, less capable than he could be. For various reasons, however, this does not follow. One is confronted many times too often by his insistence upon brilliance of a very stupid man. It could be said with some truth that the person who asserts he needs to know no more to be fully as bright as his fellows, would, upon examination, be discovered to be quite deficient in capability and understanding.

Earth has had many examples of this. The fascist is probably best described as a very stupid man who insists upon a status quo which is intolerable for all others, yet who believes himself to be brighter than all others. But even a fascist of the most modern sort—the fission fascist—would be the first to admit that both he and others could do a better job of being fascistic.

The basic reason for this is a simple one, almost idiotically simple. One can understand understanding, and can see that understanding can increase. Stupidity, ignorance, illness, aberration, incapability are only a fall away from understanding and are, themselves, less understanding and so are less understandable. One does not understand that he might get worse, and so does not have any great communication with people who tell him that he will get worse. The dying man believes right up to the moment of his last breath, no matter what he is saying to his doctor or family, that he is going to get better. He has no understanding of that state of nonunderstandingness called death. One can understand the understandable. One cannot understand the incomprehensible because the definition of incomprehensibility is nonunderstandability. As I said, this is an almost idiotically simple situation.

Life in its highest state is understanding. Life in its lower states is at a lower level of understanding, and where life has ceased to function and has arrived at what one might call total incapability, there is no understanding at all.

In Dianetics and Scientology we have a great deal to do with this subject called understanding. Understanding has very specific component parts. These component parts are affinity, reality and communication.

Affinity, reality and communication form an interdependent triangle. It is easily discovered on some inspection that one cannot communicate in the absence of reality and affinity. Further, one cannot have a reality with something with which he cannot communicate and for which he feels no affinity. And similarly, one has no affinity for something on which he has no reality and on which he cannot communicate. Even more narrowly, one does not have affinity for those things on which he has no reality and which he cannot communicate upon, and one has no reality on things which he has no affinity for and cannot communicate upon, and one cannot communicate upon things which have no reality to him and for which he has no affinity.

A graphic example of this would be anger. One becomes angry and what one says does not then communicate to the person at whom one might be angry. Even more crudely, the fastest way to go out of communication with a machine would be to cease to feel any affinity for it, and to refuse to have any reality upon it.

We call this triangle the ARC triangle. The precision definitions of these three items are as follows:

1. **Communication** is the interchange of ideas or particles between two points. More precisely, the definition of communication is: cause, distance, effect with intention and attention and a duplication at effect of what emanates from cause.

2. **Reality** is the degree of agreement reached by two ends of a communication line. In essence, it is the degree of duplication achieved between cause and effect. That which is real is real simply because it is agreed upon, and for no other reason.

3. **Affinity** is the relative distance and similarity of the two ends of a communication line. Affinity has in it a mass connotation. The word itself implies that the greatest affinity there could be would be the occupation of the same space, and this, by experiment, has become demonstrated. When things do not occupy the same space their affinity is delineated[1] by the relative distance and the degree of duplication.

---

1. **delineated:** outlined or described.

These three items, affinity, reality and communication, can be demonstrated to equate into understanding. Above understanding is knowingness without formula or design, and this might be considered to be a unit activity. Dropping down from a complete knowingness we would arrive into the realm of understanding, for this is a third dynamic manifestation peculiar to two or more individuals. Were you to be a clever mathematician, you could discover by symbolic logic[2] how all mathematical formulas could be derived from this principle that understanding is composed of affinity, reality and communication. No mathematics falling outside this triangle is a valid mathematics to man. There is no additional factor in understanding except significance, but this, of course, is the idea or consideration mentioned in the communication formula (1, above).

It is a truism that if we could understand all life we would then tolerate all life. Further, and more germane to ability, if one could occupy the position of any part of life, one would feel a sufficient affinity for life to be able to merge with it or separate from it at will.

When we say "life" all of us know more or less what we are talking about, but when we use this word *life* practically, we must examine its purposes and behavior, and in particular the formulas evolved by life in order to have a game called "life."

When we say "life" we mean understanding, and when we say "understanding" we mean affinity, reality and communication. To understand all would be to live at the highest level of potential action and ability. The quality of life exists in the presence of understanding—in the presence, then, of affinity, reality and communication. Life would exist to a far less active degree in the levels of misunderstanding, incomprehensibility,

---

2. **symbolic logic:** a system for applying the principles of mathematics to logical reasoning, using symbols to represent exact relationships between concepts.

psychosomatic illness and physical and mental incapabilities. Because life is understanding it attempts to understand. When it turns and faces the incomprehensible it feels balked and baffled, feels there is a secret, and feels that the secret is a threat to existence.

A secret is antipathetic to life, and therefore life, in searching for those things which would seem to reduce it, will hit upon various secrets it must discover. The basic secret is that a secret is an absence of life, and a total secret would be a total unlivingness.

Now let us look at this formula of communication and discover that we must have a duplication at effect of what emanates from cause. The classic example here is a telegram sent from New York City to San Francisco which says "I love you." When it arrives in San Francisco the machinery of communication has perverted it so that it says "I loathe you." This failure of duplication is looked upon as an error, and would cause considerable problems and trouble. It could not, then, be considered to be a very good communication. There was nothing wrong with the basic intention. There was nothing wrong with the attention which would be given the wire in San Francisco. The only thing that was wrong was a failure to duplicate at effect what emanated at cause.

Now if life is understanding it would find it very, very difficult to communicate with something which was nonunderstanding. In other words, life, faced with a nonunderstanding thing, would feel itself balked, for life, being understanding, could not then become nonunderstanding without assuming the role of being incomprehensible. Thus it is that the seeker after secrets, unless his way is carefully wended,[3] is trapped into being a secret himself.

---

3. **wended:** traveled.

Where one has an effect point which is an incomprehensible thing, and where one is occupying the cause point, in order to get any communication through to the effect point at all, it would be necessary for the one at cause point to somehow or another reduce his understandingness down toward incomprehensibility. The salesman knows this trick very well. He looks at his customer, recognizes his customer is interested in golf, and then pretends to be interested in golf himself in order to have the customer receive his sales talk. The salesman establishes points of agreement and potential duplication, and then proceeds into a communication. Thus searchers after truth have often walked only into labyrinths of untruth—secrets—and have themselves become incomprehensible, with conclusions of incomprehensibility. Thus we have the state of beingness of the philosophic textbooks of earth. A wonderful example of this is Immanuel Kant,[4] the Great Chinaman of Königsburg, whose German participial phrases and adverbial clauses, and whose entire reversal of opinion between his first and second book balks all our understanding as it has the understanding of philosophic students since the late eighteenth century. But the very fact that it is incomprehensible has made it endure, for life feels challenged by this thing which, pretending to be understanding, is yet an incomprehensibility. This is the grave into which so many philosophers walk. This is the coffin into which the mathematician, seeking by mathematics the secrets of the universe, eventually nails himself. But there is no reason why anyone should suffer simply because he looks at a few secrets. The test here is whether or not an individual possesses the power to be at his *own* determinism. If one can determine himself to be incomprehensible at will, he can of course, then, determine himself to be comprehensible again. But if he is obsessively, and without understanding, being determined into incomprehensibilities,

---

4. **Kant, Immanuel:** (1724–1804) German philosopher, said that man had a section of knowledge called unknowable.

then of course he is lost. Thus we discover that the only trap into which life can fall is to do things without knowing it is doing them. Thus we get to a further delineation of the secret and we discover that the secret, or any secret, could exist only when life determined to face it without knowing and without understanding that it had so determined this action. The very best grade secret, then, would be something which made life also tend to forget that it was looking at a secret.

One can always understand that his ability can increase, because in the direction of an increase of ability is further understanding. Ability is dependent entirely upon a greater and better understanding of that field or area in which one cares to be more able. When one attempts to understand less ability he is, of course, looking at less comprehensibility, less understanding, and so does not then understand lessening ability anywhere near as well as he understands increasing ability. In the absence of understanding of ability we get a fear of loss of ability, which is simply the fear of an unknown, or a thought-to-be-unknowable thing, for there is less knownness and less understanding in less ability.

Because life does not want to face things which are less like life, one has a tendency to resist and restrain itself from confronting the less comprehensible. It is this resistance alone which brings about the dwindling spiral,[5] the descent into this less ability. Life does not will this descent into less ability unless life is cognizant of the principles involved. Life resists itself into this less ability. There is a primary rule working here: That which one

---

5. **dwindling spiral:** a phenomenon of the ARC triangle whereby when one breaks some affinity, a little bit of the reality goes down, and then communication goes down, which makes it impossible to get affinity as high as before; so a little bit more gets knocked off affinity, and then reality goes down, and then communication. This is the dwindling spiral in progress, until it hits the bottom—death—which is no affinity, no communication and no reality.

fears, one becomes. When one refuses to duplicate something, and yet remains in its environment, his very resistance to the thing he refuses to duplicate will cause him eventually to become possessed of so many energy pictures of that thing, which he refuses to duplicate, that he will, to have any mass at all, find himself in possession of those energy pictures; and, without actually noticing what has happened, is very likely to accept, at their level, those things which he refused to duplicate earlier. Thus we get the riddle of the engram, the facsimile, if we understand, at the same time, that life does not necessarily find it bad to have masses of energy around, and is, indeed, unhappy unless it does have some energy. For if there is no energy, then there is no game. Life has a motto that any game is better than no game. It has another motto: Any havingness[6] is better than no havingness. Thus we find individuals clutching to them the most complex and destructive of facsimiles and mechanisms. They do not necessarily want these complexities, and yet they want the energy or the game which these complexities would seem to offer them.

If you would make anyone well, you must then concentrate upon an increase of ability, an increase of understanding. The only reason bad things come to life is because understanding has impressed further life into them. When an individual faces some secret, the fact that he is facing it and injecting life into it alone causes the secret to activate and have force and action. The only way a bad situation in existence can continue to have life is by taking life from nearby sources of communication. The bad things of life, then, have life only to that degree that understanding is invested in them. We have an example in poliomyelitis,[7]

---

6. **havingness:** the concept of being able to reach. By *havingness* is meant owning, possessing, being capable of commanding, taking charge of objects, energies and spaces.

7. **poliomyelitis:** inflammation of the gray matter of the spinal cord. Certain forms of the disease produce muscular paralysis and atrophy, others do not.

which was at one time an extremely minor and unheard-of illness. By various publications, by a great deal of advertising, by many invitations to combat this illness, it was made to take prominence and manifest itself in the society. The only life, actually, which poliomyelitis has is the amount of life which can be invested in poliomyelitis. Yet, poliomyelitis, one thinks, would exist and continue its way if it were ignored. If one were to go on ignoring poliomyelitis, now that one knows about poliomyelitis, yes, this would be the case. The disease would continue to exist although everyone was studiously ignoring it. As a matter of fact it would get worse. If, however, it were to be completely understood, and if an ability on the part of individuals existed by which they could face it without having to resist it, then the matter would be solved.

One wonders why all the nurses and doctors in contagious wards do not immediately pick up the illness, and here we have another factor which is the same factor as understanding, but couched in a different way. People do not acquire obsessively those things which they do not fear. An individual has to resist something, has to be afraid of something, has to be afraid of the consequences of something before it can have any adverse obsessive effect upon him. At any time he could have a self-determined duplication of it, but this, not being obsessive, not being against his will, would of course not produce any ill symptom beyond the length of time he determined it.

Part of understanding and ability is control. Of course, it is not necessary to control everything everywhere if one totally understands them. However, in a lesser understanding of things, and, of course, in the spirit of having a game, control becomes a necessary factor. The anatomy of control is start, stop and change, and this is fully as important to know as understanding itself, and as the triangle which composes understanding: affinity, reality and communication.

The doctors and nurses in a contagious ward have some feeling of control over the illnesses which they see before them. It is only when they begin to recognize their inability to handle these ills or these patients that they, themselves, succumb to this. In view of the fact that of recent centuries we have been very successful in handling contagious diseases, doctors and nurses, then, can walk with impunity through contagious wards.

The fighters of disease, having some measure of control over the disease, are then no longer afraid of the disease, and so it cannot affect them. Of course, there would be a level of body understanding on this which might yet still mirror fear, but we would have the same statement obtaining. People who are able to control something do not need to be afraid of it, and do not suffer ill effects from it. People who cannot control things can receive bad effects from those things.

Here we have an example of what might happen in the realm of disease. How about human aberration? We discover that the sanitariums of the world are all too often inhabited, in addition to patients, by those persons who were formerly at work in these institutions. It is a rather shocking thing to discover in ward nine the nurse who was once supervisor of a mental hospital. Now, here we had a condition where there was no control or understanding. People did not understand mental illness, aberration, insanity, neurosis. The first actual effort along this line which cut down the tally was Freudian Analysis,[8] and

---

8. **Freudian Analysis:** Freud's methods in psychoanalysis. Psychoanalysis: a system of mental therapy developed by Sigmund Freud [(1856–1939) Austrian physician and neurologist; founder of psychoanalysis] in Austria in 1894 and which depends upon the following practices for its effects: the patient is made to talk about and recall his childhood for years while the practitioner brings about a transfer of the patient's personality to his own and searches for hidden sexual incidents believed by Freud to be the only cause of aberration; the practitioner reads sexual significances into all statements and evaluates them for the patient along sexual lines. Each of these points later proved to be based on false premises and incomplete research, accounting for their lack of results and the subsequent failure of the subject and its offshoots.

yet this, requiring much too long, was not an effective weapon. These doctors and nurses in institutions who, then, are themselves patients in the same institutions knew definitely that they did not have any real control over insanity. Thus, having no control over it, they became subject to it. They could not start, stop and change insanity. The franticness of this state is represented by the medieval torture which has been utilized in such institutions as "cures." By "cured" the people in charge of such institutions merely meant "quieter." The natural course of existence would lead them to think in terms of euthanasia,[9] and so they have—that it would be best to kill the patient rather than to have his insanity continue. And they have even accomplished this at the rate of two thousand mental patients a year dead under electric shock machines. And they have accomplished it by a very high percentage dead under brain operations. The only effectiveness of electric shock and brain operations would be to render the patient less alive and more dead, and the end product, of death, achieved so many times would of course be the only way to stop the insanity. These people, of course, could not envision the fact that immortality and insanity in a future generation would crop up as a problem. They had to conceive that if they killed a patient, or simply made him much quieter, they had then triumphed to some degree. In view of the fact that man, sane or insane, is not to be destroyed according to law weighs against this "solution."

With Dianetics, to use the study in a relatively narrow field of application, we have assumed some control over insanity, neurosis, aberration, and can actually start, stop and change aberration. In the first book, *Dianetics: The Modern Science of Mental Health*, techniques were present which would place in

---

9. **euthanasia:** the original definition of *euthanasia* is "mercy killing" or "easy death." However, under the practice of psychiatry it has become "the act of killing people considered a burden on society."

view, and then vanquish them, almost any mental manifestation known in the field of insanity and aberration. Where an auditor was unable to do anything for the insane or the neurotic, the fault (if fault there was) generally lay in the fact that the auditor was actually afraid. His fear was born entirely out of his insecurity in starting, stopping and changing the condition.

In modern instruction at Academies of Scientology, there is little or no emphasis placed upon the case of the student, and yet when the student graduates he is discovered to be in a very high tone. The entire concentration is upon giving the student the ability to handle any and all types of case, and he becomes sufficiently secure in his ability—if he is graduated—to walk without any fear and with considerable calm through areas of psychosis, neurosis, and physical illness. He has been given the technologies by which these misbehaviors of life can be controlled. In view of the fact that he can start, stop and change them he need no longer fear them, and could with impunity work around the insane if this were his mission.

The handling of psychosis, neurosis and psychosomatic illness do not happen to be the mission of the auditor. Indeed, these things get well only if they are more or less ignored. As long as the accent is upon ability any malfunction will eventually vanish. The mission of the auditor is in the direction of ability. If he increases the general ability of the preclear in any and all fields, then, of course, any misabilities such as those represented by psychosis, neurosis and psychosomatic illness will vanish. The auditor, however, is not even covertly interested in these manifestations. Around him he sees a world which could be far more able. It is his business to make it so. While business, in general, does not recognize there is anything wrong with its abilities, it can recognize that its abilities can be better. One well-trained auditor working with Group Processing on the United States Air Force could treble the number of pilots successfully graduated from the schools, and could reduce the crash toll of high-speed planes by fully three-quarters. This is not a wild statement. It is simply an application of the research data already to hand. The mission is greater ability, not an eradication of inability.

Just to give more understanding to those around him could be said to be a sufficient mission for a well-trained auditor, for by doing so he would certainly increase their ability. By increasing their ability he would be able to increase their life. The common denominator[10] of all neurosis, psychosis, aberration and psychosomatic ills is "can't work." Any nation which has a high incidence of these is reduced in production, is reduced in longevity.*

*(Amongst the unable is the criminal, who is unable to think of the other fellow, unable to determine his own actions, is unable to, follow orders, unable to make things grow, is unable to determine the difference between good and evil, is unable to think at all or the future — Anybody has some of these the criminal has all of them — L

---

10. **common denominator:** a quality, attribute, opinion, etc., shared by all the persons or things in a group.

And what does one do about "how bad it is"? Well, if one depends for a long time upon others or the environment to do something about it, or depends upon force, he will fail. From his viewpoint the only one who can put more life, more understanding, more tolerance and more capability into the environment is himself, just by existing in a state of higher understanding. Without even being active in the field of auditing, just by being more capable, an individual could resolve for those around him many of their problems and difficulties.

The accent is on ability.

5

The
Auditor's Code

5

The Auditor's Code

There are several codes in Scientology and Dianetics. The only one which has to be obeyed if we wish to obtain results upon a preclear is the Auditor's Code, 1954. In the first book, *Dianetics: The Modern Science of Mental Health*, we had an Auditor's Code which was derived more or less from an ideal rather than from practical experience. In the ensuing years a great deal of auditing has been done and a great many errors have been made by auditors. And when we have taken the common denominator of what has caused preclears to make small or negative progress, we discover that these can be codified so as to inform the auditor, who wishes to get results, what to avoid in his processing.

When a psychoanalyst or psychologist uses Dianetics he is very prone to be operating in his own frame of conduct. It is the conduct of the practitioner almost as much as the processes which makes Dianetics work. In psychoanalysis, for instance, we discover that the basic failure of Freud's work in practice and as used by analysts fails chiefly because of two things done by the analyst in the consultation room. Whatever the value of Freud's libido theory,[1] the effectiveness is reduced by the analyst's evaluation for the patient. The patient is not allowed to work out his

---

1. **libido theory:** a theory originated in 1894 by Sigmund Freud which states that all life impulses and behaviors are sex-motivated.

own problems, or come to his own conclusions. He is given ready-made interpretations. In psychology there is no operating code, for clinical psychology is not much practiced and is, indeed, outlawed in many states. While psychiatry might have a modus operandi,[2] none of those conversant with this handling of the insane—the function of psychiatry—would call it a code intended to induce a better state of beingness in a patient.

In education, which is in itself a therapy, we discover an almost total absence of codified conduct beyond that laid down by school boards to regulate the social attitude of and restrain the possible cruelty in educators. Although education is very widespread, and indeed is the practice best accepted by this society for the betterment of individuals, it yet lacks any tightly agreed-upon method or conduct codification for the relaying of data to the student. Custom has dictated a certain politeness on the part of the professor or teacher. It is generally believed to be necessary to examine with rigor and thoroughness. Students are not supposed to whisper or chew gum, but education in general has no code designed to oil the flow of data from the rostrum[3] to the student bench. On the contrary, a great many students would declare that any existing code was designed to stop any flow whatever.

Dianetics is in an interesting position in that it is itself; and although people may try to classify it with mental therapy, it is closer to the level of education so far as the society itself is concerned. Its goal is the improvement of the mind on a self-determined basis, and its intended use is upon individuals and groups. Because it was an accumulation of data which is apparently the agreed-upon factors from which existence is

---

2. **modus operandi:** mode of operation; way of doing or making; procedure.

3. **rostrum:** any platform, stage, etc., for public speaking.

constructed, and although the simple perusal[4] of this data very often frees an individual, it is also disseminated on an individual and group basis directly to individuals and groups, and is a form of self-recognition.

If you were to make the best progress along any highway you would do well to follow its signs. In the Auditor's Code of 1954 we have a number of signposts, and if their directions are pursued, a maximum of result will result. If they are not pursued, one is liable to find the preclear over in the ditch in need of a tow truck in the form of a better auditor. Quite in addition to the command of the processes themselves, the difference between the book auditor[5] and the professional auditor lies in the observance of this code. A very great deal of time is invested in the auditor at Academies of Scientology in demonstrating to him the effects of disobedience of this code and obedience of it, and in leading him to practice it closely. This supervision in Academies is relatively simple. One takes a look at the class and finds somebody who is not in good shape. One discovers who audited him, and one then knows what auditor is not following the Auditor's Code. The offending student is then taken aside and briefed once more. A graduating auditor has to know this code by heart, and more importantly has to be able to practice it with the same unconscious ease as a pilot flies a plane.

The Auditor's Code, 1954

1. Do not evaluate[6] for the preclear.
2. Do not invalidate or correct the preclear's data.

---

4. **perusal:** the act of reading.

5. **book auditor:** someone who has successfully applied Scientology from a book to help someone else and who has been certified for doing so.

6. **evaluate:** to impose data or knowledge upon another. An example would be someone telling another why he is the way he is instead of permitting or guiding him to discover it for himself.

3. Use the processes which improve the preclear's case.

4. Keep all appointments once made.

5. Do not process a preclear after 10:00 P.M.

6. Do not process a preclear who is improperly fed.

7. Do not permit a frequent change of auditors.

8. Do not sympathize with the preclear.

9. Never permit the preclear to end the session on his own independent decision.

10. Never walk off from a preclear during a session.

11. Never get angry with a preclear.

12. Always reduce every communication lag[7] encountered by continued use of the same question or process.

13. Always continue a process as long as it produces change, and no longer.

14. Be willing to grant beingness to the preclear.

15. Never mix the processes of Dianetics with those of various other practices.

16. Maintain two-way communication with the preclear.

This is actually the Auditor's Code, 1954, amended, since it has one additional clause from the original release of this code — number 16: Maintain two-way communication with the preclear.

If one were to sort out these various provisos[8] he would discover all of them important, but that three of them were more vitally concerned with processing than the others, and that these three, if overlooked, would inevitably and always result in case failure. These three are the differences between a good auditor and a bad auditor. They are numbers 12, 13 and 16.

---

7. **communication lag:** the length of time intervening between the posing of the question, or origination of a statement, and the exact moment that question or original statement is answered.

8. **provisos:** conditions or stipulations.

In 12 we discover that the auditor should reduce every communication lag encountered by continued use of the same question or process. Almost every case failure contains some of this. The difference between a professional auditor and a book auditor is most visible in this and the other two provisos mentioned. A good auditor would understand what a communication lag is—the length of time intervening between the asking of the question and the receiving of a direct answer to that question, regardless of what takes place in the interval—and he would be very careful to use only those processes on the preclear which the preclear could reasonably answer up to, and he would be very certain not to walk off from a communication lag into which the session had entered. A bad auditor would believe, when he had struck a communication lag, that he had simply found a blind alley,[9] and would hastily change to some other question.

In number 13, "Always continue a process as long as it produces change, and no longer," we find the greatest frailty on the part of auditors. An auditor who is not in good condition or who is not well trained will "Q and A"[10] with the preclear. When the preclear starts to change, the auditor will change the process. (By *Q and A* we mean that the answer to the question is the question, and we indicate a duplication.) Here we find an auditor, possibly so much under the command of the preclear, rather than the reverse, that the auditor simply duplicates obsessively what the preclear is doing. The preclear starts to change, therefore the auditor changes. A process should be run as long as

---

9. **blind alley:** a situation offering no chance for progress or improvement.

10. **Q and A:** the practice of asking a question about a pc's answer, i.e., the auditor asks a question, the pc answers, the auditor asks a question about the answer. This is the chief auditor fault, as it is giving session control over to the pc. The auditor following only the pc's lead is giving no auditing and the pc is left on "self-audit." Here is a wrong example of auditing: *Auditor:* "How are you?" *Pc:* "Awful." *Auditor:* "What's wrong?" Here is a right example: *Auditor:* "How are you?" *Pc:* "Awful." *Auditor:* "Thank you."

it produces change. If the preclear is changing that is what the auditor wants. If the auditor were to stop and change off to some other process just because the preclear had attained some change, we would discover some very sick preclears. Additionally, an auditor is liable to continue a process long after it has stopped producing change. He and the preclear get into a sort of a marathon, a machine-motivated grind, on Opening Procedure by Duplication,[11] which probably after ten hours produced no further alteration in the preclear. Yet, this pair might go on to fifty hours with the process and would be quite disheartened to discover that for forty hours nothing had happened. This, however, is much less harmful as an action than the changing of the process simply because it is producing change.

The maintenance of a two-way communication is the most touchy activity in auditing. An auditor being the auditor and being concentrated upon controlling the preclear, all too often forgets to listen when the preclear speaks. Many an auditor is so intent upon the process that when it produces a change which the preclear thinks he should advise upon, the auditor ignores him. Ignoring the preclear at a time when he wishes to impart some vital information generally sends the preclear directly into apathy. At the same time, an auditor should not permit a preclear to keep on talking forever, as in the case of a lady recently reported who talked to the auditor for three days and three nights. The therapeutic value of this was zero, for the auditor was listening to the machine, not to a preclear. One should understand rather thoroughly the difference between an obsessive or compulsive communication line and an actual communication. Listening to circuits of course validates circuits. The

---

11. **Opening Procedure by Duplication:** a Scientology process. It has as its goal the separating of time, moment from moment. This is done by getting a preclear to duplicate his same action over and over again with two dissimilar objects. In England this process is called "Book and Bottle," probably because these two familiar objects are the most used in doing Opening Procedure by Duplication.

---

auditor should pay attention to the rational, the usual, the agreed-upon, and should leave very much alone the bizarre, the freakish, the compulsive and the obsessive manifestations of the preclear. The maintenance of a two-way communication is actually a process in itself, and is the first, most basic process of Dianetics, and continues on through all remaining processes.

Simply because we have pinpointed three of these is no reason to ignore the others. Every time there has been a "psychotic break" by reason of or during auditing, it has occurred when the processing was being done late at night, when the preclear was improperly fed, when the preclear had had a frequent change of auditors, and when two-way communication had not been maintained and the effort on the part of the preclear to impart a vital change to the auditor was ignored. All these "psychotic breaks" were repaired, but because these factors were present the patching up was rather difficult. Audit them early, audit them bright, listen to what they have to say about what's happening, make sure they are eating regularly, and change auditors on a preclear as seldom as possible, and no psychotic breaks will occur.

If you are simply investigating Dianetics to discover whether or not it is workable, you should be aware of the fact that the Auditor's Code, following of, is an essential portion of Dianetics. Dianetics functions very poorly in the absence of the Auditor's Code. It is part of the process, not simply a polite way to go about handling people. Thus, if Dianetics is tested in the absence of the Auditor's Code, do not pretend that it has been tested at all.

Another phrase might have been added to this code, but it would be more germane to living than to auditing, and that phrase would be "Maintain silence around unconscious or semi-conscious people." The reason for this is contained in *Dianetics:*

The Modern Science of Mental Health and in Preventive Dianetics. Such statements become "engramic." The addition of this to the Auditor's Code, however, is not practical, for the auditor often finds himself talking to a "groggy" preclear. Because the auditor is reducing every communication lag he encounters by the repetition of the question, the asking of a question or giving of a command to a semiconscious preclear is thus rendered relatively unaberrative, for sooner or later the question embedded in the unconsciousness will work loose, and, indeed, the communication lag will not flatten until this occurs. Thus, simply the reduction of the communication lag in itself eradicates such phrases. Thus, this is not part of the Auditor's Code. However, when we encounter unconsciousness or semiconsciousness, as in moments immediately after the injury of a child, a street accident, an operation, we maintain silence for we are not auditing the person. Mothers and fathers would spare themselves a great deal of later mental unrest on the child's part if they knew and would follow this injunction, and in many other ways it is a very important one. A man can be killed by too much conversation around him while he is injured. No matter how deeply unconscious he may appear to be, something is always registering. The questioning by police at the scene of an accident, where the person being questioned is in a state of shock, or where other accident victims are present, is probably the most aberrative conduct in this society. The questioning by police is quite restimulative in any event, and many severe complications after accidents have been traced immediately to this activity on the part of the police. It might be very important for some ledger somewhere to know exactly who caused this. It is more important that the people involved in it live and be happy afterwards. It is not that we do not like police. This is not the case. We simply believe that police should be civilized, too.

Simply memorizing this code is not enough. Memorizing it in order to practice it is indicated, but it is the practice of this code which is important. Observance of it is the hallmark of a good auditor, and it signalizes[12] the recovery of the case.

If an auditor is going to raise the ability of the preclear, his ability in the field of auditing must be considerable. That ability begins with the understanding and observance of the Auditor's Code, 1954, amended.

---

12. **signalizes:** makes clearly known; draws attention to.

6

Trapped

6

Trapped

In Greece, Rome, England, colonial America, France and Washington, a great deal of conversation is made on the subject of freedom. Freedom, apparently, is something that is very desirable. Indeed, freedom is seen to be the goal of a nation or a people. Similarly, if we are restoring ability to the preclear we must restore freedom. If we do not restore freedom we cannot restore ability. The muscle-bound wrestler, the tense driver, the rocket jockey[1] with a frozen reaction time alike are not able. Their ability lies in an increase of freedom, a release of tension, and a better communication to their environment.

The main trouble with freedom is it does not have an anatomy. Something that is free is free. It is not free with wires, vias, bypasses or dams, it is simply free. There is something else about freedom which is intensely interesting: it cannot be erased. In *Dianetics: The Modern Science of Mental Health* we learned that pleasure moments were not erasable. The only thing that was erasable was pain, discomfort, distortion, tenseness, agony, unconsciousness. In more modern Scientological parlance, freedom cannot be "as-ised,"[2] it is something which is

---

1. **rocket jockey:** an astronaut.

2. **as-ised:** viewed exactly as it is, without any distortions or lies, at which moment it vanishes and ceases to exist.

imperishable. You may be able to concentrate somebody's attention on something that is not free and thus bring him into a state of belief that freedom does not exist, but this does not mean that you have erased the individual's freedom. You have not. All the freedom he ever had is still there. Furthermore, freedom has no quantity, and by definition it has no location in space or time. Thus we see the awareness of awareness unit as potentially the freest thing there could be. Thus man's concentration upon freedom.

But if freedom has no anatomy, then please explain how one is going to attain to something which cannot be fully explained? If anyone talks about a road to freedom he is talking about a linear line. This, then, must have boundaries. If there are boundaries there is no freedom. This brings the interesting proposition to mind that the very best process, by theory, would be to have an individual assume himself to be free, and then he would simply be asked to assume himself to be free again. Indeed, on many cases of high-toned variety, this is a quite workable process. An individual is sick, he is usually in very good tone, the auditor simply asks him to assume that he is free, and he will cease to be sick. This magic, however, is limited to those people who have some concept of what *free* means. Talk to a person who works from eight o'clock until five with no goals, with no future or no belief in the organization or its goals, who is being required by time payments, rent and other barriers of an economic variety to invest all of his salary as soon as it is paid, and we have an individual who has lost the notion of freedom. His concentration is so thoroughly fixed upon barriers that freedom has to be in terms of less barriers. Thus, in processing we have to audit in the direction of less and less barriers in order to attain freedom.

If freedom is so very compelling and is so useful, and is in itself something like a synonym for ability—even if not entirely—

then it is our task to understand a little more about freedom as itself in order to accomplish its attainment, for unfortunately it is not enough to the bulk of the human race simply to say "be free" and have the individual recover.

Life is prone to a stupidity in many cases in which it is not cognizant of a disaster until the disaster has occurred. The middle western farmer had a phrase for it: "Lock the door after the horse is stolen." It takes a disaster in order to educate people into the existence of such a disaster. This is education by pain, by impact, by punishment. Therefore, a population which is faced with a one-shot disaster which will obliterate the sphere would not have a chance to learn very much about the sphere before it was obliterated. Thus, if they insisted upon learning by experience in order to prevent such a disaster, they would never have the opportunity. If no atomic bomb of any kind had been dropped in World War II, it is probable there would be no slightest concern about atomic fission, although atomic fission might have developed right on up to the planet-buster without ever being used against man, and then as a planet-buster being used on Earth, so destroying it.

If a person did not know what a tiger was, and we desired to demonstrate to him that no tigers were present, we would have a difficult time of it. Here we have a freedom from tigers without knowing anything about tigers. Before he could understand an absence of tigers he would have to understand a presence of tigers. This is the process of learning we know as "by experience."

In order to know anything, if we are going to use educational methods, it is necessary then to know, as well, its opposite. The opposite of tigers probably exists in Malayan jungles where tigers are so frequent that the absence of tigers would be a novelty, indeed. A country which was totally burdened by tigers might not understand at all the idea that there were no tigers in some parts of the world, and a great deal of argument would have to be entered into with the populace of a tiger-burdened area to get them to get any inkling of what an absence of tigers would be. Many cases in processing have suddenly lost a somatic, to discover themselves in a new and novel state. This somatic was so routine and so constant and so pervasive that they could not intellectually conceive of what life would be like without that particular somatic.

The understanding of freedom, then, is slightly complex in that individuals who do not have it are not likely to understand it, and thus we find an individual who knows nothing about exteriorization and knows everything about being in constant contact with the sensations of a body failing to grasp the idea of the freedom resulting from exteriorization. These people do not even believe that exteriorization can exist, and so combat it. They are so little experienced on the subject of freedom that this type of freedom is "known to be nonexistent" to them.

The way to demonstrate the existence of freedom is to invite the individual to experience freedom, but if he does not know what freedom is, then he will not exteriorize. We have to hit some sort of a gradient scale on the matter, or make him turn around and look squarely at the opposite of freedom.

But the opposite of freedom is slavery—everybody knows this—or is it? I do not think these two things are a dichotomy. Freedom is not the plus of the condition where slavery is the minus unless we are dealing entirely with the political organism. Where we are dealing with the individual, better terminology is necessary and more understanding of the anatomy of minus-freedom is required.

Minus-freedom is entrapment. Freedom is the absence of

barriers. Less freedom is the presence of barriers. Entirely minus-freedom would be the omnipresence of barriers. A barrier is matter or energy or time or space. The more matter, energy, time and space assumes command over the individual the less freedom that individual has. This is best understood as entrapment since slavery connotes an intention, and entrapment might be considered almost without intention. A person who falls into a bear pit might not have intended to fall into it at all, and the bear pit might not have intended a person to fall upon its stake. Nevertheless, an entrapment has occurred. The person is in the bear pit.

If one wants to understand existence and his unhappiness with it, he must understand entrapment and its mechanisms.

In what can a person become entrapped? Basically and foremost, he can become entrapped in ideas. In view of the fact that freedom and ability can be seen to be somewhat synonymous, then ideas of disability are first and foremost in entrapment. I dare say, amongst men the incident has occurred that a person has been sitting upon a bare plain in the total belief that he is entirely entrapped by a fence. There is that incident mentioned in *Self Analysis* of fishing in Lake Tanganyika[3] where the sun's rays, being equatorial, pierce burningly to the lake's bottom. The natives there fish by tying a number of slats of wood on a long piece of line. They take either end of this line and put it in canoes, and then paddle the two canoes to shore, the slatted line stretching between. The sun shining downward presses the shadows of these bars down to the bottom of the lake and thus a cage of shadows moves inward toward the shallows. The fish seeing this cage contract upon them, which is composed of nothing but the absence of light, flounder frantically into the

---

3. **Lake Tanganyika:** lake in east central Africa 420 miles long, between 30 and 45 miles wide with a maximum depth of 4710 feet.

shallows where they cannot swim and are thus caught, picked up in baskets and cooked. Yet there was nothing to be afraid of but shadows.

When we move out of mechanics, man finds himself on unsure ground. The idea that ideas can be so strong and pervasive is foreign to most men. For instance, a government attacked by the communists does not perceive that it is being attacked only by ideas. It believes itself to be attacked by guns, bombs, armies and yet it sees no guns, bombs, armies. It sees only men standing together exchanging ideas. Whether these ideas are sound or not is beside the point, they are at least penetrative. No sixteen-inch armor plate could possibly stop an idea. Thus a country can be entrapped, taken and turned toward communism simply by the spread of the communistic idea. A country that fails to understand this arms itself, keeps its guns cocked, its armies alert, and then succumbs at last to the idea now entered into the head of the armed forces, which it so hopefully employed. The collapse of Germany in World War I was an instance of this. Its armies, its grand fleet were all flying the red flag. Although Allied pressure and the conditions of starvation in Germany had much to do with this defeat, nevertheless, it was keyed into being by this communist idea infiltrated into the minds of the men who originally were armed and trained to protect Germany. And communism, just as an idea, traps the minds of men. They find themselves organized into cells, they find their customs abandoned and a regimented, militant, biological, soulless tyranny their master. Here is an idea becoming a sort of trap.

So first and foremost, we have the idea. Then, themselves the product of ideas, we have the more obvious mechanics of entrapment in matter, energy, space and time.

The most common barrier which man recognizes as such

would be a wall. This is so obviously a barrier that individuals quite commonly suppose all barriers to be composed of solid walls. However, almost any object can be made into a barrier. A less common use of an object as a barrier would be one which inhibited, by some sort of suction or drag, a departure from it. A solid lump of considerable magnetic properties will hold to it a piece of steel. Gravity is, then, a barrier of a kind. It holds the people or life units of Earth to Earth.

Another barrier would be energy. A sheet of energy or something carrying energy, such as an electrical fence, can prove to be a formidable barrier. A cloud of radioactive particles obstructing passage into another space would also be a barrier. Tractor-type beams,[4] as in the case of gravity, could be seen to be a barrier of sorts, but in the form of energy.

Yet another barrier, easily understood, is that of space. Too much space will always make a barrier. Space debars an individual from progressing into another part of the galaxy. One of the finest prisons one could imagine would be one located on a small piece of matter surrounded by such a quantity of space that no one could cross it. Space is such an efficient barrier that people in the Southwest of the United States, committing crimes discover their way everywhere blocked by the giganticness of space. In New York City it would be very easy for them, after the commission of the crime, to vanish, but in attempting to cross a space of such size as the Southwest they become exposed everywhere to view, there being nothing else on which the police can fix their attention.

Quite another barrier, less well understood but extremely thorough, is the barrier of time. Time debars your passage into the year 1776 and prevents your repossession of things which

---

4. **tractor-type beams:** energy flows that pull things toward their source.

you had in your youth. It also prevents you from having things in the future. Time is an exceedingly effective barrier. The absence of time can also be a barrier, for here an individual is unable to execute his desires and is so constricted by the pressure of time itself.

Matter, energy, space and time can all, then, be barriers. An awareness of awareness unit, however, which is the personality and beingness of the person, and which is composed of quality, not quantity, can be anywhere it wishes to be. There is no wall thick enough, nor any space wide enough, to debar the reappearance at some other point of an awareness of awareness unit. In that this *is* the individual, and not some ghost of the individual, and as the individual is himself an awareness of awareness unit and not his machinery and his body, we see that as soon as one understands completely that he is an awareness of awareness unit, he no longer is restricted by barriers. Thus, those who would seek entrapment for individuals are entirely antipathetic toward the idea of exteriorization, and a person who knows nothing but barriers is apt to believe that a condition of no-barriers could not exist. Yet a condition of no-barriers can exist, and this is itself freedom.

Examining freedom, then, we have to examine why people do not attain it easily or understand it. They do not attain freedom because their attention is fixed upon barriers. They look at the wall, not the space on either side of the wall. They have entities and demon circuits which demand their attention, and indeed, the body itself could be considered to be an attention-demanding organism. One might believe that its total function was to command interest and attention. It is so interesting that people do not conceive that just behind them lies all the freedom anybody ever desired. They even go so far as to believe that that freedom is not desirable and that if they could attain it they would not want it. One is reminded of prisoners who occasionally go so sufficiently "stir-crazy"[5] as to demand, after their release from prison, confining walls and restricted spaces. Manuel Komroff[6] once wrote a very appealing story on this subject, the story of an old man who had served twenty-five years in prison, or some such time, and who on his release asked for nothing more than the smallest room in his son's house and was happiest when he could see someone on an opposite roof who had the appearance of a guard, and who actively put bars back on his window. One could consider that a person who has been for a long time in a body to have such a fixation upon the barriers imposed by the body, that once an auditor tries to remove them the preclear puts them back quickly. You might say such a person is "stir-crazy," yet the condition is remediable.

The anatomy of entrapment is an interesting one, and the reason why people get entrapped and, indeed, the total mechanics of entrapment are now understood. In Scientology a great deal of experimentation was undertaken to determine the factors which resulted in entrapment, and it was discovered that the answer to the entire problem was two-way communication.

Roughly, the laws back of this are: Fixation occurs only in the presence of one-way communication. Entrapment occurs only when one has not given or received answers to the thing entrapping him. Thus we see the ARC triangle itself, and most importantly the communication factor of that triangle, looming up to give us a roadway to freedom.

It could be said that all the entrapment there is, is the waiting one does for an answer.

---

5. **stir-crazy:** mentally ill because of long imprisonment.

6. **Komroff, Manuel:** (1890–1974) American writer born in New York City.

Here we find man. Basically he is an awareness of awareness unit which is capable of, and active in, the production of matter, energy, space and time as well as ideas. We discover that he is more and more fixated upon ideas, matter, energy, space and time and the processes and functions involving these. And we discover that these, being the product of the awareness of awareness unit, do not supply answers to the awareness of awareness unit unless the awareness of awareness unit supplies itself those answers.

Entrapment is the opposite of freedom. A person who is not free is trapped. He may be trapped by an idea, he may be trapped by matter, he may be trapped by energy, he may be trapped by space, he may be trapped by time, and he may be trapped by all of them. The more thoroughly the preclear is trapped the less free he is. He cannot change, he cannot move, he cannot communicate, he cannot feel affinity and reality. Death itself could be said to be man's ultimate in entrapment. When a man is totally entrapped he is dead.

It is our task in investigation and auditing to discover for the individual and the group the roadway to a greater freedom, which is the roadway to a greater ability.

The processes the auditor uses today are designed entirely to secure greater freedom for the individual, for the group, for mankind. Any process which leads to a greater freedom for all dynamics is a good process. It should be remembered, however, that an individual functions on all dynamics, and that the suppression by the individual of the third or fourth dynamic leads to less freedom for the individual himself. Thus, the criminal, becoming immorally free, harms the group and harms mankind, and thus becomes less free himself. Thus there is no freedom in the absence of affinity, agreement and communication. Where an individual falls away from these his freedom is sharply curtailed and he finds himself confronted with barriers of magnitude.

The component parts of freedom, as we first gaze upon it, are, then, affinity, reality and communication, which summate into understanding. Once understanding is attained, freedom is obtained. For the individual who is thoroughly snarled in the mechanics of entrapment, it is necessary to restore to him sufficient communication to permit his ascendance into a higher state of understanding. Once this has been accomplished his entrapment is ended.

None of this is actually a very difficult problem and the auditing done today is very simple. But where the auditing is done by a person who does not basically desire the freedom of the individual a further entrapment is more likely to ensue than further freedom. The obsessively entrapped are then enemies of the preclear, for they will trap others.

A greater freedom can be attained by the individual. The individual does desire a greater freedom, once he has some inkling of it. And auditing according to the precision rules and codes of Dianetics and Scientology steers the individual out of the first areas of entrapment to a point where he can gain higher levels of freedom, either by further auditing or by himself. The only reason we need a regimen[7] with which to begin is to start an individual out of a mirror-maze of such complexity that he himself, in attempting to wend his way, only gets lost.

This is Dianetics 1955!

---

7. **regimen:** a certain, settled schedule of things.

7

Communication

7

Communication

Communication is so thoroughly important today in Dianetics and Scientology, as it always has been on the whole track, that it could be said if you were to get a preclear into communication you would get him well. This factor is not new in psychotherapy, but concentration upon it is new, and interpretation of ability as communication is entirely new.

If you were to be in thorough and complete communication with a car and a road, you would certainly have no difficulty driving that car. But if you are in only partial communication with the car and in no communication with the road, it is fairly certain that an accident will occur. Most accidents do occur when the driver is distracted by an argument he has had, or by an arrest, or a white cross alongside the road that says where some motorist got killed, or by his own fears of accidents.

When we say somebody should be in present time we mean he should be in communication with his environment. We mean, further, that he should be in communication with his environment as it exists, not as it existed. And when we speak of prediction we mean that he should be in communication with his environment as it will exist, as well as as it exists.

If communication is so important, what is communication?

It is best expressed as its formula, which has been isolated, and by use of which a great many interesting results can be brought about in ability changes.

There are two kinds of communication, both depending upon the viewpoint assumed. There is outflowing communication and inflowing communication. A person who is talking to somebody else is communicating to that person (we trust), and the person who is being talked to is receiving communication from that person. Now, as the conversation changes, we find the person who has been talked to is now doing the talking, and is talking to the first person, who is now receiving communication from him.

A conversation is the process of alternating outflowing and inflowing communication, and right here exists the oddity which makes aberration and entrapment. There is a basic rule here: He who would outflow must inflow—he who would inflow must outflow. When we find this rule overbalanced in either direction we discover difficulty. A person who is only outflowing communication is actually not communicating at all in the fullest sense of the word, for in order to communicate entirely he would have to inflow as well as outflow. A person who is inflowing communication entirely is again out of order, for if he would inflow he must then outflow. Any and all objections anyone has to social and human relationships is to be found basically in this rule of communication, where it is disobeyed. Anyone who is talking, if he is not in a compulsive or obsessive state of beingness, is dismayed when he does not get answers. Similarly, anyone who is being talked to is dismayed when he is not given an opportunity to give his replies.

Even hypnotism can be understood by this rule of communication. Hypnotism is a continuing inflow without an opportunity on the part of the subject to outflow. This is carried on to such a degree in hypnotism that the individual is actually trapped in the spot where he is being hypnotized, and will remain trapped in that spot to some degree from there on. Thus, one might go so far as to say that a bullet's arrival is a heavy sort of hypnotism. The individual receiving a bullet does not outflow a bullet, and thus he is injured. If he could outflow a bullet immediately after receiving a bullet, we can introduce the interesting question, "Would he be wounded?" According to our rule he would not be. Indeed, if he were in perfect communication with his environment he could not even receive a bullet injuriously. But let us look at this from a highly practical viewpoint.

As we look at two life units in communication we can label one of them "a" and the other one of them "b." In a good state of communication "a" would outflow and "b" would receive, then "b" would outflow and "a" would receive. Then "a" would outflow and "b" would receive. Then "b" would outflow and "a" would receive. In each case both "a" and "b" would know that the communication was being received and would know what and where was the source of the communication.

All right, we have "a" and "b" facing each other in a communication. "A" outflows. His message goes across a distance to "b" who inflows. In this phase of the communication "a" *is* Cause, "b" is Effect, and the intervening space we term the Distance. It is noteworthy that "a" and "b" are both life units. A true communication is between two life units. It is not between two objects, or from one object to one life unit. "A," a life unit, is cause. The intervening space is distance. "B," a life unit, is effect. Now a completion of this communication changes the roles. Replied to, "a" is now the effect, and "b" is the cause. Thus we have a cycle which completes a true communication. The cycle is cause, distance, effect, with effect then becoming cause and communicating across a distance to the original source, which is now effect, and this we call a two-way communication.

As we examine this further we find out that there are other factors involved. There is "a's" intention. This, at "b" becomes attention, and for a true communication to take place, a duplication at "b" must take place of what emanated from "a." "A," of course, to emanate a communication, must have given attention, originally, to "b," and "b" must have given to this communication some intention, at least to listen or receive; so we have both cause and effect having intention and attention.

Now, there is another factor which is very important. This is the factor of duplication. We could express this as reality, or we could express it as agreement. The degree of agreement reached between "a" and "b" in this communication cycle becomes their reality, and this is accomplished mechanically by duplication. In other words, the degree of reality reached in this communication cycle depends upon the amount of duplication. "B" as effect, must to some degree duplicate what emanated from "a" as cause, in order for the first part of the cycle to take effect, and then "a," now as effect, must duplicate what emanated from "b" for the communication to be concluded. If this is done there is no aberrative consequence. If this duplication does not take place at "b" and then at "a" we get what amounts to an unfinished cycle of action. If, for instance, "b" did not vaguely duplicate what emanated from "a" the first part of the cycle of communication was not achieved, and a great deal of randomity, explanation, argument, might result. Then if "a" did not duplicate what emanated from "b" when "b" was cause on the second cycle, again an uncompleted cycle of communication occurred with consequent unreality. Now naturally, if we cut down reality, we will cut down affinity. So where duplication is absent affinity is seen to drop. A complete cycle of communication will result in high affinity and will, in effect, erase itself. If we disarrange any of these factors we get an incomplete cycle of communication and we have either "a" or "b" or both *waiting* for the end of cycle. In such a wise the communication becomes aberrative.

The word *aberrate* means to make something diverge from a straight line. The word comes basically from optics. Aberration is simply something which does not contain straight lines. A confusion is a bundle of crooked lines. A mass is no more and no less than a confusion of mismanaged communications. The energy masses and deposits, the facsimiles and engrams surrounding the preclear are no more and no less than unfinished cycles of communication which yet wait for their proper answers at "a" and "b."

An unfinished cycle of communication generates what might be called "answer hunger." An individual who is waiting for a signal that his communication has been received is prone to accept any inflow. When an individual has, for a very long period of time, consistently waited for answers which did not arrive, any sort of answer from anywhere will be pulled in to him, by him, as an effort to remedy his scarcity for answers. Thus he will throw engramic phrases in the bank into action and operation against himself.

Uncompleted cycles of communication bring about a scarcity of answers. It does not much matter what the answers were or would be as long as they vaguely approximate the subject at hand. It does matter when some entirely unlooked-for answer is given, as in compulsive or obsessive communication, or when no answer is given at all.

Communication itself is aberrative only when the emanating communication at cause was sudden and *non sequitur*[1] to the environment. Here we have violations of attention and intention.

The factor of interest also enters here but is far less important, at least from the standpoint of the auditor. Nevertheless, it

---

1. **non sequitur:** not following; an unrelated or illogical statement or conclusion.

explains a great deal about human behavior, and explains considerable about circuits. "A" has the intention of interesting "b." "B," to be talked to, becomes interest*ing*. Similarly "b," when he emanates a communication, is interest*ed* and "a" is interest*ing*. Here we have, as part of the communication formula (but as I said, a less important part) the continuous shift from being interest*ed* to being interest*ing* on the part of either of the terminals, "a" or "b." Cause is interest*ed*, effect is interest*ing*.

Of some greater importance is the fact that the intention to be received, on the part of "a" places upon "a" the necessity of being duplicatable. If "a" cannot be duplicatable in any degree, then, of course, his communication will not be received at "b," for "b," unable to duplicate "a," cannot receive the communication. As an example of this, "a," let us say, speaks in Chinese, where "b" can only understand French. It is necessary for "a" to make himself duplicatable by speaking French to "b" who only understands French. In a case where "a" speaks one language, and "b" another, and they have no language in common, we have the factor of mimicry possible and a communication can yet take place. "A," supposing he had a hand, could raise his hand. "B," supposing he had one, could raise his hand. Then "b" could raise his other hand, and "a" could raise his other hand, and we would have completed a cycle of communication by mimicry. Communication by mimicry could also be called communication in terms of mass.

We see that reality is the degree of duplication between cause and effect. Affinity is monitored by intention and the particle sizes involved, as well as the distance. The greatest affinity there is for anything is to occupy its same space. As the distance widens affinity drops. Further, as the amount of mass or energy particles increases, so again does affinity drop. Further, as the velocity departs from what "a" and "b" have considered optimum velocity—either greater or lesser velocity than what they consider to be the proper velocity—affinity drops.

There is another fine point about communication, and that is expectancy.

Basically, all things are considerations. We consider that things are, and so they are. The idea is always senior to the mechanics of energy, space, time, mass. It would be possible to have entirely different ideas about communication than these. However, these happen to be the ideas of communication which are in common in this universe, and which are utilized by the life units of this universe. Here we have the basic agreement upon the subject of communication in the communication formula as given here. Because ideas are senior to this, a thetan can get, in addition to the communication formula, a peculiar idea concerning just exactly how communication should be conducted, and if this is not generally agreed upon, can find himself definitely out of communication. Let us take the example of a modernistic writer who insists that the first three letters of every word should be dropped, or that no sentence should be finished, or that the description of characters should be held to a cubist[2] rendition. He will not attain agreement among his readers and so will become to some degree an "only one." There is a continuous action of natural selection, one might say, which weeds out strange or peculiar communication ideas. People, to be in communication, adhere to the basic rules as given here, and when anyone tries to depart too widely from these rules, they simply do not duplicate him and so, in effect, he goes out of communication.

We have seen an entire race of philosophers go out of existence since 1790. We have seen philosophy become a very

---

2. **cubist:** refers to *cubism,* a technique of writing that attempts to exploit abstract structural relationships of things by using bizarre associations and dissociations in imagery, the simultaneous evocation of several points of view toward the material, and other devices.

unimportant subject, where once it was a very common coin[3] among the people. The philosophers themselves put themselves out of communication with the people by insisting on using words of special definition which could not be assimilated with readiness by persons in general. The currency of philosophy could not be duplicated by those with relatively limited vocabularies. Take such jaw-cracking[4] words as *telekinesis.*[5] While it probably means something very interesting and very vital, if you will think back carefully no taxi driver has mentioned the word to you while you were paying your fare, or even during the more verbose moments of the ride. Probably the basic trouble with philosophy was that it became Germanic in its grammar, an example set by Immanuel Kant. And if you will recall that wonderful story by Saki,[6] a man was once trampled to death while trying to teach an elephant German irregular verbs. Philosophy shed some of its responsibility for a cycle of communication by rendering itself unduplicatable by its readers. It is the responsibility of anyone who would communicate that he speak with such vocabulary as can be understood. Thus philosophy did not even begin for some hundred and fifty years a sound cycle of communication, and thus is dead.

Now let us take up the individual who has become very "experienced" in life. This individual has a time track in particular. His time track is his own time track, it isn't anyone else's time track. The basic individualities among men are based upon the fact that they have different things happen to them and that

---

3. **common coin:** something that is current through being commonly mentioned, discussed or accepted.

4. **jaw-cracking:** hard to pronounce.

5. **telekinesis:** the ability to move or deform inanimate objects through mental processes.

6. **Saki:** pen name for Hector Hugo Munro (1870–1916), English short story writer and novelist, known for his witty, often bizarre stories.

they view these different things from different points of view. Thus we have individualization and we have individual opinion, consideration and experience. Two men walking down the street witness an accident. Each one of them sees the accident from at least a slightly different point of view. Consulting twelve different witnesses of the same accident, you are likely to find twelve different accidents. Completely aside from the fact that witnesses like to tell you what they think they saw instead of what they saw, there were actually twelve different points from which the accident was viewed, and so twelve different aspects of the occurrences. If these twelve were brought together, and if they were to communicate among themselves about this accident, they would then reach a point of agreement on what actually happened. This might not have been the accident, but it certainly is the agreed-upon accident, which then becomes the real accident. This is the way juries conduct themselves. They might or might not be passing upon the real crime, but they are certainly passing upon an agreed-upon crime.

In any war it takes two or three days for enough agreement to occur to know what took place in a battle. Whereas there might have been a real battle, a real sequence of incidents and occurrences, the fact that every man in the battle saw the battle from his own particular point of view, by which we mean severely "point from which he was looking," rather than his opinions—no one saw the battle in its entirety. Thus, time must intervene for enough communication on the subject of the battle to take place so that all have some semblance of agreement on what occurred. Of course, when the historians get to this battle and start writing different accounts of it, out of the memoirs of generals who were trying to explain away their defeats, we get a highly distorted account indeed. And yet this becomes the agreed-upon battle, as far as history is concerned. Reading the historians one realizes one will never really know what took place at Waterloo,[7] at Bennington,[8] at Marathon.[9] In that we can consider as a communication one soldier shooting at another soldier, we see that we are studying communications about communications. This scholarly activity is all very nice, but does not carry us very far toward the resolution of human problems.

We have seen these two words *cause* and *effect* playing a prominent role in the communication formula. We have seen that first cause became at the end of the cycle last effect. Furthermore, the intermediate point, first effect, immediately changed to cause in order to have a good communication cycle. What, then, do we mean by cause? Cause is simply the point of emanation of the communication. What is effect? Effect is the receipt point of the communication. In that we are only interested in life units, we see that we can readily ascertain cause at any time. We are not interested in secondary or tertiary cause. We are not interested in assisting causes in any way. We are not interested in secondary and tertiary effects. We are not interested in assisting effects in any way. We consider any time that we look at a source point of a communication that we are looking at cause. In that the entire track is composed of this pattern of cause and effect, an individual is very prone, whenever he sees a possible cause point, to look for an earlier cause point, and then an earlier one, and an earlier one, and an earlier one, and after a while takes to reading the Bible, which is very hard on the eyesight.

In view of the fact that all cause is simply elected cause, and all effect is simply elected effect, and that the primary echelon is

---

7. **Waterloo:** a battle on 18 June 1815, near the town of Waterloo, in central Belgium, in which the British and the Prussians decisively defeated Napoleon and ended his power.

8. **Bennington:** a battle of the American Revolutionary War in which U.S. troops defeated the British. It was fought in 1777 near Bennington, Vermont.

9. **Marathon:** a plain in southeast Greece where the Athenians defeated the Persians in 490 B.C.

the idea level of communication, that is cause which we elect to be cause, that is effect which elects to be effect, and there is no more that can be said about it. *Cause* in our dictionary here means only source point. *Effect* means only receipt point.

We notice that the receipt point, midway in the cycle of communication, shifts and becomes source point. We could classify this shift in this center of the cycle of communication in some other fashion, but it is not necessary to do so. We would be getting too particular for our purposes.

Now we come to the problem of what a life unit must be willing to experience in order to communicate. In the first place the primary cause point must be willing to be duplicatable. It must be able to give at least some attention to the receipt point. The primary receipt point must be willing to duplicate, must be willing to receive, and must be willing to change into a source point in order to send the communication, or an answer to it, back. And the primary source point in its turn must be willing to be a receipt point. As we are dealing basically with ideas and not mechanics, we see, then, that a state of mind must exist between a cause and effect point whereby each one is willing to be cause or effect at will, is willing to duplicate at will, is willing to be duplicatable at will, is willing to change at will, is willing to experience the distance between, and, in short, willing to communicate. Where we get these conditions in an individual or a group we have sane people. Where an unwillingness to send or receive communications occurs, where people obsessively or compulsively send communications without direction and without trying to be duplicatable, where individuals in receipt of communication stand silent and do not acknowledge or reply, we have aberrative factors. And it is very interesting to note from the standpoint of processing, that we have all the aberrative factors there are. We do not need to know anything further about aberration than that it is a disarrangement of the cycle of communication. But to know that, of course, we have to know the component parts of communication and the expected behavior.

Some of the conditions which can occur in an aberrated line are a failure to be duplicatable before one emanates a communication, an intention contrary to being received, an unwillingness to receive or duplicate a communication, an unwillingness to experience distance, an unwillingness to change, an unwillingness to give attention, an unwillingness to express intention, an unwillingness to acknowledge, and, in general, an unwillingness to duplicate. We might go so far as to say that the reason communication takes place instead of occupying the same space and knowing—for communication introduces the idea of distance—is that one is unwilling to *be* to the degree necessary to be anything. One would rather communicate than be. Thus we find that the inability to communicate is a gradient scale—that goes down along with the inability to be. We get individuals winding up as only willing to be themselves, whatever that is, and thus becoming "the only one." To the degree that a person becomes "the only one" he is unwilling to communicate on the remaining dynamics. An individual who has become only himself is in a sad and sorry plight of being off the second, third, and fourth dynamics, at least.

It might be seen by someone that the solution to communication is not to communicate. One might say that if he hadn't communicated in the first place he wouldn't be in trouble now. Perhaps there is some truth in this, but there is more truth in the fact that processing in the direction of making communication unnecessary, or reducing communication, is not processing at all, but murder. A man is as dead as he can't communicate. He is as alive as he can communicate. With countless tests in the Hubbard Association of Scientologists International[10] department

---

10. **Hubbard Association of Scientologists International (HASI):** the general membership group of the church at the time of this book. It was open to individuals who

of writing and investigation, I have discovered to a degree which could be called conclusive, that the only remedy for livingness is further communicatingness. One must add to his ability to communicate.

Probably the only major error which exists in Eastern philosophy, and probably the one at which I balked when I was young, was this idea that one should withdraw from life. It seemed to me that every good friend I had among the priests and holy men was seeking to pull back and cut off his communications with existence. Whatever the textbooks of Eastern philosophy may say, this was the practice of the people who were best conversant with Eastern mental and spiritual know-how. Thus I saw individuals taking fourteen or eighteen years in order to get up to a high level of spiritualistic serenity. I saw a great many men studying and very few arriving. To my impatient and possibly practical Western viewpoint this was intolerable. For a very great many years I asked this question, "To communicate, or not to communicate?" If one got himself in such thorough trouble by communication, then of course one should stop communicating. But this is not the case. If one gets himself into trouble by communicating, he should further communicate. More communication, not less, is the answer, and I consider this riddle solved after a quarter of a century of investigation and pondering.

used Scientology procedures to improve themselves and others. It has since been replaced as a membership group by the International Association of Scientologists (IAS). At the time this book was written, the HASI also handled the publication of materials, provided professional training and processing services and additionally functioned as a research and investigation unit.

8

The Application of Communication

8

The Application of Communication

If you think we are talking about anything very esoteric, or highly mathematical, kindly read the communication formula again. Just because we are speaking of the basic fundamentals of sanity, aberration, freedom, ability, truth, knowledge and secrets is no reason why we have to be complicated. We expect the fundamentals of behavior to be complicated simply because so many highly complicated people have discussed the subject. If Immanuel Kant couldn't, and if Adler[1] addled communication, there is no reason why we should.

As we speak of the applications of communication we are speaking of complexities of these fundamentals, and having isolated the fundamentals, we do not then see any complexity in the product of the basics. Let us say that we thoroughly understand that two plus two equals four. Now we write this on a piece of paper and put it on a table. It is still understandable. Now we write on another piece of paper two plus two equals four and put it on the same table. Now on a third piece of paper we write two plus two equals four and add it to those on the

---

1. **Adler:** Alfred Adler (1870–1937) Viennese psychologist who opposed Freud's emphasis on sex and advanced his own theory of the inferiority complex to explain psychopathic cases.

table. We take four tablets full of paper and on each sheet we write two plus two equals four, and tearing each sheet out, add these. Now we get some blocks of wood, and we write two plus two equals four on these blocks of wood. We get some leather and charcoal and write two plus two equals four, and add that to the table. Then we get some blackboards, and on each one write two plus two equals four and put them on the table. And we get some colored chalk and write two plus two equals four in various colors on another blackboard and put it on the table. Then we have two plus two equals four bound in vellum and add that to the pile on the table. Then we get some building bricks and we scratch on them two plus two equals four and put them on the table. Now we get four gallons of ink and pour it over two plus two equals four, and smear everything we have put on the table. Now we take a bulldozer and push the table out through the wall. We take a steamroller and run over the debris. We take some concrete and pour it over the whole and let it dry, and we still have not altered the fact that two plus two equals four.

In other words, no matter what mechanics we add to the communication formula, no matter what form we use to communicate, no matter how many types of words and meanings we place into the communication formula to become messages, no matter how we scramble meanings, messages, cause points and effect points, we still have the communication formula.

Here we have an individual. He has been living for a many-evented lifetime. He began life, let us say, with a perfect grasp of the communication formula. His experience has been consistent departures from the communication formula only to the degree that he failed to emanate or failed to receive, twisted, perverted or failed to return communications, and at the end of that lifetime all we would have to do to put him into excellent condition would be to restore in its complete clarity his ability to execute the communication formula. The only thing which has happened to him has been violation of the communication formula. He emanated something. It was not received. When it was received it was not acknowledged. When it replied he did not receive it. And thus he begins to look further and further afield for communications and becomes more and more complicated in his view of communications, becomes less and less duplicatable, is less and less able to duplicate; his intentions swerve further and further, his attention becomes more and more altered. What should have been straight lines wind up in a ball, and we have our preclear after a lifetime of living with *Homo sapiens*. All we have to do to get him into the most desirable clarity would be to restore his ability to perform the various parts of the communication formula and his ability to apply that formula to anything in this or any universe. He would have to be willing to duplicate anything. He would have to be willing to make himself duplicatable. He would have to be able to tolerate distance and velocities and masses. He would have to be able to form his own intentions. He would have to be able to give and receive attention. He would have to take or leave at will the intentions of others, and more important, he would have to be at any point and make it a cause or receipt point at will. If he were able to do this he could not possibly be trapped, for here we are intimately walking into the deepest secret of a trap.

What is a secret? It is the answer which was never given, and this is all a secret is. Thus knowledge and use of the communication formula within the framework of Dianetics and Scientology resolves any and all secrets and even the belief in secrets.

The only thing which could be said to aberrate communication would be restriction or fear of restriction. A person who is not communicating is one who has restricted communication. A person who is communicating compulsively is afraid of being restricted in his communication. A person who is talking on another subject than that to which cause was giving his attention has been so restricted on the subject of communication elsewhere, or has experienced such a scarcity of communication elsewhere, that he is still involved with communication elsewhere. This is what we mean by "not in present time."

When we look at problems, without which humanity cannot seem to live, we discover that a problem is no more and no less than a confusion of communication lines, missing cause or effect points, undeterminable distances, misread intentions, missing attentions, and failures in the ability to duplicate and be duplicatable. Move off the communication formula in any direction and a problem will result. A problem, by definition, is something without an answer. Not because the two words are similar, but because all of humanity has confused them, we find that answer to a communication and answer to a problem can, for our purposes, be synonymous.

When one has failed to get answers consistently to his communications, he begins to run into a scarcity for answers, and he will get problems in order to have solutions, but he will not solve any of the problems because he already has a scarcity of answers. An auditor walks in on a preclear who has a scarcity of answers, finds the preclear has a circuit of problems, tries to resolve some of the problems of the preclear, discovers that the preclear creates new problems faster than old ones can be resolved. The one thing the preclear knows is that there aren't any answers—not to his particular kind of problems. He knows this to such a degree that he is unable to conceive of answers, which means to him that he is unable to conceive of solutions. He is like the old man in Manuel Komroff's story who, after his release from prison, yet created a cell of his own. He cannot look at freedom. He does not believe freedom exists. He cannot envision a world without tigers. The remedy for this, of course, is to have him remedy his lack of answers by having him mock up[2] answers.

That confused look you see on a mathematician's face is the task he has set himself to procure symbolic answers to hypothetical abstracts,[3] none of which, of course, are human answers. The longer he symbolizes, the more formulas he creates, the further he drifts from the human race. Answers are answers only when they come from living units. All else is a glut[4] on the market. No mathematical formula ever gave anybody any answer to anything unless it was to the problem of communication itself, but this I invite your attention, was not involved with, and was not derived from, mathematics as we know them. The communication formula was derived from an observation of and working with life. It could be derived only because one had entirely abandoned the idea that energy could tell anyone anything. Life is not energy. Energy is the byproduct of life.

Your recluse is one who has become so thoroughly convinced that there are no obtainable answers from anyone that he does no longer believe that life itself exists. He is the only living thing alive, in his opinion. Why? Because he is the only thing which communicates. I dare say every recluse, every "only one," every obsessively or compulsively communicating individual, has so thoroughly associated with "life units" which were so dead that it became "very plain" that no one else was alive.

The attitude of the child toward the adult contains the opinion that adults have very little life in them. A child, with his enthusiasms, is in his family everywhere surrounded by communication blocks of greater or lesser magnitude. His questions do

---

2. **mock up:** knowingly create a mental image picture that is not part of the time track.

3. **abstracts:** ideas or terms considered apart from some material basis or objects.

4. **glut:** a supply of certain goods that is greater than the demand.

not get answered. The communications which are addressed to him are not posed in a way which can be duplicated. In other words, the adult does not make himself duplicatable. Freud and his confreres were entirely in error in believing that the child is totally self-centered. It is not the child who is totally self-centered. He believes that he is in communication with the total world. Investigation of children demonstrates that they are very heavy on the first, second, third and fourth dynamics. The child is so convinced of his ability to communicate that he will touch a hot stove. Life has no terrors for him. He has not yet learned by experience that he cannot communicate. It's the adult who has drawn back into the "only one" and one believes that the inspiration of this continuous belief on the part of the psychologist and psychoanalyst that the child is entirely self-centered and has only his own world must be the expression of an opinion held by the psychoanalyst and psychologist out of his own bank. As one grows one goes less and less into communication with the environment until he is at last entirely out of it. Only he is out of it in the wrong direction—dead.

Where you see aberration, where you would wish to detect aberration, you must look for violations in the communication formula. People who consistently and continuously violate portions of the communication formula can be suspected of being just that dead. The further one departs from the communication formula the more death exists for them. The more concentrated they become on secrets, the more they question intentions, the less they are likely to assume the point of view called cause or the point of view called effect.

One should not go so far as to say that life is communication. It is, however, a native condition of life to be able to communicate. Life, the awareness of awareness unit, the ability to have unlimited quality with no quantity, or to produce quantity, is capable of communication. And here again we are consulting ability. Ability, first and foremost, could be conceived to be the ability to *be*, and also the ability to vary beingness, and this means the ability to communicate. One has to be able to be in order to communicate. One has to be able to vary one's beingness in order to return communications.

There is the manifestation, then, known as the "stuck flow." This is one-way communication. The flow can be stuck incoming or it can be stuck outgoing. The part of the communication cycle which goes from primary cause to effect may be the flow that is stuck, or it might be the other from "b" back to "a" that is stuck. Here we have several possible methods of achieving a stuck flow, and several conditions of flow, four to be exact. The flow can be stuck from primary cause to effect, from the viewpoint of primary cause. The flow can be stuck from primary cause to primary effect from the viewpoint of primary effect. The flow can be stuck from effect-turned-cause to final effect, from the viewpoint of effect-turned-cause. The flow can be stuck from effect-turned-cause to final effect, from the viewpoint of final effect. These four stuck flows can become—any of them or a combination of them—the anatomy of the communication lag of the case. A person can hear but cannot answer. A person can cause a communication to begin, but cannot receive an acknowledgment. A primary cause can be totally engrossed in keeping the flow from arriving at primary effect, and so forth.

A failure to complete a cycle of communication will leave some part of that communication in suspense. It will leave it, in other words, silent, and this will stick on the track. It will float in time. It will restimulate. It will attract and hold attention long after it has occurred.

Unconsciousness itself results from receipt of too much, too heavy communication. It can similarly, but less often, result from the emanation of too much, too heavy communication as in the case of blowing up a large balloon, where one becomes dizzy after the expulsion of too much breath. Theoretically, one sending a large mass toward another one might fall unconscious as a result of sending too much mass away from himself too suddenly, and we find this can be the case. This is degradation because of loss. Ones gives away too much, or loses too much, and the departure of the mass, or even the idea, can bring about a drop in consciousness. In view of the fact that a thetan can create at will, this is not a very dangerous situation. One can receive too much communication too suddenly, such as a cannonball. Unconsciousness will result from this. Most engrams are composed of too much incoming mass and too much outgoing mass so as to make a confusion into which any answer, any phrase interjected can then be effective since there is a scarcity of phrases and a plus in masses. One could even go so far as to say that the only reason a mass interchange is ever effective in the line of unconsciousness is that it does not have enough reasons with it. I suppose if one explained carefully enough to a soldier why he had to be shot, the arrival of the bullet would not make him unconscious or hurt him. But again this is theoretical, since very little reason goes on in war and thus it has never been subjected to a clinical experiment.

The resolution of any stuck flow is remedying the scarcity of that which stuck the flow. This might be answers, it might be original communications, it might be chances to reply.

The communication formula at work is best understood through the "communication lag."

9

Two-Way Communication

9

Two-Way
Communication

A cycle of communication and two-way communication are actually two different things. If we examine closely the anatomy of communication we will discover that a cycle of communication is not a two-way communication in its entirety.

If you will inspect Graph "A" below, you will see a cycle of communication:

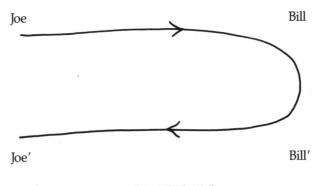

Joe   Bill

Joe'   Bill'

GRAPH "A"

Here we have Joe as the originator of a communication. It is his primary impulse. This impulse is addressed to Bill. We find Bill receiving it, and then Bill originating an answer or acknowledgment as Bill', which acknowledgment is sent back to Joe'. Joe has said, for instance, "How are you?" Bill has received this, and then Bill (becoming secondary cause) has replied to it as Bill', with "I'm okay," which goes back to Joe', and thus ends the cycle.

Now what we call a two-way cycle of communication may ensue as in Graph "B" below:

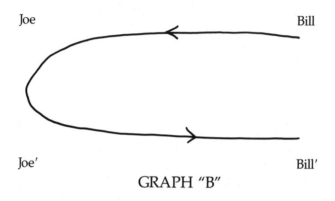

Joe   Bill

Joe'   Bill'

GRAPH "B"

Here we have Bill originating a communication. Bill says, "How's tricks?" Joe receives this, and then as Joe' or secondary cause, answers "Okay, I guess," which answer is then acknowledged in its receipt by Bill'.

In both of these graphs we discover that in Graph "A" the acknowledgment of the secondary cause was expressed by Joe' as a nod or a look of satisfaction. And again, in Graph "B" Joe's' "Okay, I guess" is actually acknowledged by Bill' with a nod or some expression signifying the receipt of the communication.

If both Joe and Bill are "strong, silent men" (highly aberrated), they would omit some portion of these cycles. The most flagrant omission and the one most often understood as "communication lag" by the auditor would be for Joe in Graph "A" to say "How are you?" and for Bill to stand there without speaking. Here we have Joe causing a communication, and Bill' failing to continue the cycle. We do not know or inquire, and we are not interested in, whether or not Bill as the receipt point ever did hear it. We can assume that he was at least present, and that Joe spoke loudly enough to be heard, and that Bill's attention was somewhere in Joe's vicinity. Now, instead of getting on with the cycle of communication, Joe is left there with an incompleted cycle and never gets an opportunity to become Joe'.

There are several ways in which a cycle of communication could not be completed, and these could be categorized as:

1. Joe failing to emanate a communication,

2. Bill failing to hear the communication,

3. Bill' failing to reply to the communication received by him, and

4. Joe' failing to acknowledge by some sign or word that he has heard Bill'.

We could assign various reasons to all this, but our purpose here is not to assign reasons why they do not complete a communication cycle. Our entire purpose is involved with the noncompletion of this communication cycle.

Now, as in Graph "A," let us say we have in Joe a person who is compulsively and continually originating communications whether he has anybody's attention or not, and whether or not these communications are germane to any existing situation. We discover that Joe is apt to be met, in his communicating, with an inattentive Bill who does not hear him, and thus an absent Bill' who does not answer him, and thus an absent Joe' who never acknowledges.

Let us examine this same situation in Graph "B." Here we

have, in Bill, an origination of a communication. We have the same Joe with a compulsive outflow. Bill says, "How are you?" and the cycle is not completed because Joe, so intent upon his own compulsive line, does not become Joe' and never gives Bill a chance to become Bill' and acknowledge.

Now let us take another situation. We find Joe originating communications, and Bill a person who never originates communications. Joe is not necessarily compulsive or obsessive in originating communications, but Bill is aberratedly inhibited in originating communications. We find that Joe and Bill, working together, then get into this kind of an activity: Joe originates communication, Bill hears it, becomes Bill', replies to it, and permits Joe a chance to become Joe'. This goes on quite well, but will sooner or later hit a jam on a two-way cycle, which is violated because Bill never originates communication.

A two-way cycle of communication would work as follows: Joe, having originated a communication, and having completed it, may then wait for Bill to originate a communication to Joe, thus completing the remainder of the two-way cycle of communication. Bill does originate a communication, this is heard by Joe, answered by Joe' and acknowledged by Bill'.

Thus we get the normal cycle of a communication between two terminals, for in this case Joe is a terminal and Bill is a terminal and communication can be seen to flow between two terminals. The cycles depend on Joe originating communication, Bill hearing the communication, Bill becoming Bill' and answering the communication, Joe' acknowledging the communication, then Bill originating a communication, Joe hearing the communication, Joe' answering the communication and Bill' acknowledging the communication. If they did this, regardless of what they were talking about, they would never become in an argument and would eventually reach an agreement, even if they were hostile to one another. Their difficulties and problems would be cleared up and they would be, in relationship to each other, in good shape.

A two-way communication cycle breaks down when either terminal fails, in its turn, to originate communications. We discover that the entire society has vast difficulties along this line. They are so used to canned entertainment and so inhibited in originating communications by parents who couldn't communicate, and by education and other causes, that people get very low on communication origin. Communication origin is necessary to start a communication in the first place. Thus we find people talking mainly about things which are forced upon them by exterior causes. They see an accident, they discuss it. They see a movie, they discuss it. They wait for an exterior source to give them the occasion for a conversation. But in view of the fact that both are low on the origin of communication—which could also be stated as low on imagination—we discover that such people, dependent on exterior primal impulses, are more or less compulsive or inhibitive in communication, and thus the conversation veers rapidly and markedly and may wind up with some remarkable animosities or misconclusions. Let us suppose that lack of prime cause impulse on Joe's part has brought him into obsessive or compulsive communication, and we find that he is so busy outflowing that he never has a chance to hear anyone who speaks to him, and if he did hear them, would not answer them. Bill, on the other hand, might be so very, very, very low on primal cause (which is to say, low on communication origination) that he never even moves into Bill', or if he does, would never put forth his own opinion, thus unbalancing Joe further and further into further and further compulsive communication.

As you can see by these graphs, some novel situations could originate. There would be the matter of obsessive answering as well as inhibitive answering. An individual could spend all of his time answering, justifying or explaining—all the same thing—no primal communication having been originated at him. Another individual, as Joe' in Graph "A" or Bill' in Graph "B," might spend all of his time acknowledging, even though nothing came his way to acknowledge. The common and most noticed manifestations, however, are obsessive and compulsive origin, and nonanswering acceptance, and nonacknowledgment of answer. And at these places we can discover stuck flows.

As the only crime in the universe seems to be to communicate, and as the only saving grace of a thetan is to communicate, we can readily understand that an entanglement of communication is certain to result. What we should understand—and much more happily—is that it can now be resolved.

That which we are discussing here is minimally theory and maximally derived from observation. The main test of this is whether or not it resolves cases—and be assured that it does.

Flows become stuck on this twin cycle of communication where a scarcity occurs in:

1. origination of communication,
2. receipt of communication,
3. answering a communication given,
4. acknowledging answers.

Thus it can be seen that there are only four parts which can become aberrated in both Graph "A" and Graph "B," no matter the number of peculiar manifestations which can occur as a result thereof.

These observations of communication are so vital that a considerable difference among case results comes about between an auditor who does acknowledge whatever his preclear answers and an auditor who does not. Let us take auditor G and we discover that he is running Opening Procedure of 8-C[1] on a preclear, but that at the end of two hours of Opening Procedure of 8-C the preclear has benefited very little. Then let us take auditor K. This auditor does fifteen minutes of Opening Procedure of 8-C and gets very good results on the preclear. The difference between auditor G and auditor K is only that auditor G never acknowledges any answer or statement or communication origin on the part of the preclear. He simply continues doggedly with the process. Auditor K on the other hand, is willing to let the preclear originate a communication and always acknowledges whenever the preclear concludes the action called for in a command, or when the preclear volunteers a verbal answer. In other words, G did not answer or acknowledge but ran the process with mechanical perfection, and K both answered and acknowledged as well as originated orders. The fact that the scarcest thing there is, is the origin of orders or communications, and the fact that G was at least doing this, is enough to cause G to get some improvement in the preclear, but he will not get anything like the improvement obtained by auditor K.

Silence is nowhere desirable except only in permitting another to communicate or waiting for another to acknowledge. The auditing of silence will wind the preclear in a perfect fish net of aberration. The total process which remedies this is remedying the scarcity, by whatever means, of the four parts of a two-way communication.

---

1. **Opening Procedure of 8-C:** consists of having the preclear move his body around the room under the auditor's direction until (a) he finds he is in actual communication with many spots on the surface of things in the room, (b) until he can select spots in the room and know he is selecting them and can communicate with them, and (c) select spots and move to them, decide when to touch them and when to let go. 8-C is the number of another process and is also used to mean good control.

10

Communication Lag

10

Communication
Lag

Yesterday we used an instrument called an E-Meter[1] to register whether or not the process was still getting results so that the auditor would know how long to continue it. While the E-Meter is an interesting investigation instrument and has played its part in research, it is not today used by the auditor except perhaps in testing the basal metabolism[2] of the preclear. The E-Meter is no longer used to determine "what is wrong with the preclear." As we long ago suspected, the intervention of a mechanical gadget between the auditor and the preclear had a tendency to depersonalize the session and also gave the auditor a dependence upon the physical universe and its meters which did not have to be there. I knew when we first began to use E-Meters that sooner or later something would have to be evolved, or that something would turn up which would dispense with them. I worked along that line rather consistently and about half a year before this writing developed "communication lag" as the only diagnostic instrument needed by the auditor.*

1. **E-Meter:** an electronic device for measuring the mental state or change of state of *Homo sapiens*. It is *not* a lie detector. It does not diagnose or cure anything. It is used by auditors to assist the preclear in locating areas of spiritual distress or travail.

2. **basal metabolism:** the basic chemical change in the body between oxygen and fuel. It tells you if the preclear really is eating, or has eaten breakfast. (For further information on basal metabolism, read the book *E-Meter Essentials.*)

* Later research by L. Ron Hubbard showed that the E-Meter was vital to processing. For further information, read the books *Understanding the E-Meter, Introducing the E-Meter, E-Meter Essentials* and *The Book of E-Meter Drills.*

The exact definition of a communication lag is "the length of time intervening between the posing of the question, or origination of a statement, and the exact moment that question or original statement is answered."

If you will look very closely at this definition you will discover that nothing is said, whatever, about what goes on between the asking of the question or the origination of the communication and its being answered. What goes on in between is lag. It does not matter if the preclear stood on his head, went to the North Pole, gave a dissertation on botany,[3] stood silent, answered some other question, thought it over, attacked the auditor or began to string beads. Any other action but answering, and the time taken up by that action, is communication lag. An auditor has to understand this very thoroughly. Usually he interprets a communication lag as the length of time it takes the preclear to answer the question and loosely applies this as the length of time between the asking of the question and the first moment the preclear starts to speak. This is not communication lag, for the preclear may start to speak on some other subject, may desire more information, may *almost* answer the question, and still not actually answer the question.

If you will look around at people you will find them possessed of a great many communication lag mechanisms. In their effort not to be an effect, or in their effort not to be cause; in their aberrations about compulsive communication and inhibitive communication, and in indulging in impulsive, compulsive and inhibitive communication, they manage to assemble quite a number of interesting mechanisms. But all these mechanisms are communication lag.

3. **botany:** the science that deals with plants, their life, structure, growth, classification, etc.

Here is an example of communication lag:

Joe: "How are you, Bill?"

Bill: "You look fine, Joe."

Here the question was never answered at all and would go on as a communication lag from there until the end of the universe.

Here is another example:

Joe: "How are you, Bill?"

Bill (after twenty seconds of study): "Oh, I guess I'm all right today."

As this is the commonest form of communication lag it is the most readily observed.

Less well known is the following communication lag:

Joe: "How are you, Bill?"

Bill: "What do you want to know for?"

Again, this question goes on unanswered until the end of the universe.

The most maddening kind of communication lag is:

Joe: "How are you, Bill?"

Bill: —— silence from there on out.

This is dramatized when people anxiously inquire of an unconscious person how he is and they become entirely frantic. They are simply looking at a communication lag which they believe will become total, and their anxiety is simply their multiple suffering on the subject of communication lag.

Here is another type of communication lag:

Joe: "How are you, Bill? I was saying to Ezra the other day that I have seen a lot of sick men in my time, but you certainly look pretty bad, Bill. Now how are you? I've been down to see the doctor and he was telling me there's a lot of these colds and things going around. . . ."

In other words, Joe never gives Bill an opportunity to reply, and this is the other side of communication lag.

An auditor's understanding of the subject of communication lag is brief if he believes that it is the lag between the originator of the communication and the person to whom it is addressed. On our Graph "A" on an earlier page this would be from Joe to Bill'. There is a return lag, and that is from Bill' to Joe', and, as above, there is the lag between Joe and Joe, where Joe simply keeps on talking without ascertaining if there is any Bill' there. You could also call this return lag an "acknowledgment lag." Joe to Joe is not a communication at all. Actually, Joe to Bill' without a completion of a cycle is the same thing. Joe never acknowledges the communication and so the return lag is actually Joe to Joe. The proper sequence of such a communication is Bill' to Joe'. In other words Joe, to make a complete cycle of communication, must acknowledge in some manner, verbal or gesture, that Bill' has said something.

Joe to Joe, as a communication lag (which is to say, no acknowledgment) has as its initial root an absence, for Joe, of Bill to Bill' in Graph "B." In other words, Joe has been called upon to originate communication so consistently that he now does so compulsively and obsessively since there has been an entire scarcity of other people originating communications.

Now let us look at a highly specialized type of communication lag. Here we have Joe to Bill to Bill' to Joe', as in Graph "A."

Then we have Joe waiting for Bill, in Graph "B," to originate a communication. If Bill does not, and only silence ensues, Joe then originates another communication. In other words, we have no two-way communication.

The two-way cycle of communication is not quite as important in auditing as it would be in life, for in auditing the auditor perforce[4] is originating communications in order to get the preclear up to the point where he can originate communications. One does not remedy life by approximating it exactly in the auditing room. The process is so designed that it will accomplish a rehabilitation in life without, to a marked degree, having to live it. As an example of this, the auditor does not expect the preclear to turn around and originate some process to make the auditor well. But the auditor does expect to get audited by somebody sooner or later, or expects to be at a level where he can rise above this need of a communication interchange in order to live.

The place auditors have the most trouble with communication lag is the return lag. Auditors seldom acknowledge the execution of commands on the part of the preclear. As in Opening Procedure of 8-C—a process which is one of the six basic processes today—the auditor sends the preclear over to touch the wall. When the preclear has touched the wall, the auditor is quite prone to give another command without acknowledging the fact that the preclear has touched the wall. It is an amazing thing what the lack of acknowledgment will do to slow down a case recovery. Many times when an auditor is doing this—is acknowledging—he is doing it in such a perfunctory fashion that the preclear does not recognize it as an acknowledgment, but as a prelude to a new command. A good auditor makes very, very sure that the preclear knows the acknowledgment has occurred. As an example, the auditor says, "Go over to the wall and touch

---

4. **perforce:** by or through necessity; necessarily.

it." The preclear does so. The auditor says, "Very good," and with a definite pause after this acknowledgment says, "Now go over to that wall and touch it." In other words, the auditor who is a good auditor makes sure that the preclear knows that a complete cycle of communication has occurred on this particular auditing command.

Another failure on the part of auditors is to fail to let the preclear originate a communication. The auditor tells the preclear, "Go over to that wall and touch it." The preclear does so but stops midway in the gesture and gasps, then completes the gesture. The bad auditor will fail to note and inquire after this gasp. This is actually the origin of a communication on the part of the preclear. He does not verbalize it. He does not express it any further than some physical gesture or a look of dismay, and even these might be slight, but this is usually as far as he can go in originating a communication. The auditor who fails to pick this up fails to inform the preclear thus that the preclear is permitted to originate a communication. This gasp, this gesture, should at once be noted by the auditor with a "What's happened?" or "What's the matter?" or "Something happen?" This gives the preclear the opportunity to originate a second cycle of communication. Remember that the gesture or the gasp was actually a communication. The preclear probably will not acknowledge the auditor's statement beyond starting out on the origin of a new communication, but the fact that he does originate a statement on the subject of what is the matter is, in itself, an acknowledgment of the fact that he has heard the auditor. This is so vital that many cases have stumbled, tripped and bogged, simply because the auditor did not encourage the preclear to make a statement as to something which had occurred. Actually, the more often an auditor can do this the better auditor he is, and the more good will be done by auditing.

Now, of course, there is an opposite side to this where the

auditor can give credence to an obsessive or compulsive outflow on the part of the preclear to such an extent that the auditing is entirely interrupted. An example of this occurred recently where a preclear outflowed at an auditor three days and three nights without the auditor recognizing entirely that this was simply obsessive communication in action. But this is not communication. This is not pertinent to the situation, and the definition of compulsive or obsessive communication is "an outflow which is not pertinent to the surrounding terminals and situation." In other words, a compulsive or obsessive communication is an outflow which is not in reality with the existing reality.

We see, then, that an auditing session really does include a two-way cycle of communication, but it does not include it ever, unless the auditor invites the preclear to comment upon what is going on as he does processes.

Just as a side comment here, the way to handle an obsessive or compulsive communication is to wait for a slight break in the flow and interject an auditing command. Remember that an obsessive outflow is actually not a communication. A communication is on the subject and is in agreement with the environment. It is also in agreement with what is occurring.

Now, it doesn't happen to matter what process is being done, the basic of that process is two-way communication. In auditing, as in living, communication is existence. In the absence of communication we have silence, and where we have silence we have no time. Time is manifested in communication lag to the extent that the preclear has been subjected to silences, or such a thing as an obsessive or compulsive outflow which had nothing to do with communicating on the subject at hand, which is again a sort of silence: somebody talking obsessively or continually about things which might or might not exist, and to no one in particular without expecting any cycle of communication to take place.

A communication lag is handled by an auditor by repetition of the question or command which elicited a communication lag. Here is an example:

Bill: "How are you, Joe?"

Joe: silence, silence, silence—finally a grunt.

Bill: "How are you, Joe?"

Joe: silence, silence—"Okay, I guess."

Bill: "How are you, Joe?"

Joe: "I'm all right, I tell you!"

Bill: "How are you, Joe?"

Joe: silence—"I'm okay."

Bill: "How are you, Joe?"

Joe: "All right, I guess."

Bill: "How are you, Joe?"

Joe: "All right."

Bill: "How are you, Joe?"

Joe: "Oh, I'm all right."

This is an example of flattening a communication lag. At first we have silence and no very intelligible reply, then we have silence and a reply, and then other manifestations, each one of which demonstrates a changing interval of time until the last couple of commands—three, in actual auditing practice—where the same interval of time was present.

Flattening a communication lag requires only that the preclear answer after a uniform interval of time at least three times.

This uniform interval of time could, for practical purposes, be as long as ten seconds. Thus, we get lengths of time required to answer an auditing question as follows: answer requires thirty-five seconds; answer requires twenty seconds; answer requires forty-five seconds; answer requires twenty seconds; answer requires ten seconds; answer requires ten seconds; answer requires ten seconds. To all intents and purposes, with these three last ten second intervals the auditor could consider that he has to some degree flattened this particular auditing command because he is getting a consistent response. However, with such a long lag as ten seconds, the auditor will discover that if he asked the question two or three more times he would recover a changing interval once more.

This is the mechanical formula of flattening a communication lag. Give the order, as in Opening Procedure of 8-C, or ask the question, as in Straightwire,[5] and then continue to give that same order or ask that same question until the preclear executes it after a short interval three times the same.

There is an entirely different manifestation for a completely flattened communication lag. We get extroversion. The preclear ceases to put his attention on his mind, but puts his attention on the environment. We see this happen often in the Opening Procedure of 8-C where the preclear has the room suddenly become bright to him. He has extroverted his attention. He has come free from one of these communication tangles out of the past and has suddenly looked at the environment. This is all that has happened. On a thinkingness level this happens quite often.

---

5. **Straightwire:** the name of a process. It is the act of stringing a line between present time and some incident in the past, and stringing that line directly and without any detours. The auditor is stringing a straight "wire" of memory between the actual genus (origin) of a condition and present time, thus demonstrating that there is a difference of time and space in the condition then and the condition now, and that the preclear, conceding this difference, then rids himself of the condition or at least is able to handle it.

The preclear is doing the process very well, and then begins to remember odds and ends of appointments he has, or some such thing. Just because he does this is no reason the auditing session should be ended. It simply demonstrates an extroversion. You have, in one way or another, pulled the preclear out of a communication tangle and put him into present time when he extroverts.

Communication lag as a subject could be a very large one. We have all manner of communication lags in evidence around us. Probably the most interesting one is the shock reaction after an accident, which one occasionally sees. At times it takes the body thirty-six hours to find out and reply to the fact that it has received an impact. It is quite common for a body to suddenly manifest the impact half an hour after it. This is communication lag. There are many humorous angles to communication lag. Sometimes you ask somebody, "How are you?" and you get a reply from his social machinery. He says, "I'm fine." Then, two or three hours later, he is liable to say to you, "I feel terrible." This was the preclear, himself, answering. This was the awareness of awareness unit awakening to this communication lag.

This universe could be called a consistent and continual communication lag. One is trapped in it to the degree that he is lagging. If there were no remedy for communication lag I would never bring up the subject. However, there is, and it is a remedy which is easily undertaken in auditing today.

Entrapment is actually communication lag. One has waited for communications which never arrived, or has expected something to answer so long and so often that he becomes fixated upon something, or in something, and so does not believe he can escape from it. The first and foremost factor in communication lag, of course, is time, and the next factor is waiting, which is also dependent upon time.

As has been commented earlier, the only things which float on the time track are the moments of silence when no communication occurred. These are "no-time" moments, and so have no time in which they can live, and so they float forward on the time track. It is an oddity that an engram behaves in such a way as to put all its silent moments in present time with the preclear and leave its talking or action moments back on the track. When we took a person back to birth and ran out birth, we took out the action moments. If we did not take out, as well, the silent moments in birth, we did not take out the very things which pinned themselves to the preclear in present time. In other words, the birth engram did not move at all, but the silent moments in birth might have a tendency to come up into present time. These silent moments in engrams and facsimiles do, themselves, compose the matter extant in the preclear. This matter is not so much composed of action moments as silent moments. Thus we see that an individual, the longer he lives in this universe, the more communication lag he runs into, the more upset he is about existence, the greater his communication lag, the more he is silent. Of course, obsessive or compulsive communication is just one grade above silence. It is the last frantic effort to keep things from going entirely quiet. It is not communication and is actually silence of a sort, particularly since very few people listen to it.

Now, we are studying about communication, and we are communicating about communication, and you have every opportunity here to get yourself beautifully snarled, so I would ask you to look around your environment and check a number of manifestations of communication lag. You are not controlled by the subject. You can easily control it. The dangerous thing is not to know the answers and simply go on in these consistent and continual communication lags imposed upon us by the lack of communication in this universe.

It is of great interest to note that imagination as a function of existence becomes drowned in an absence of communication origin. An individual can become so dependent upon others or entertainments in originating communications that he himself does not. Indeed, it is very unpopular in this society at this time to originate communications. One should always say that somebody else thought of it first, or that it goes back to the ancient Ugluks, or that it's happened many times before, or that one has just dug up the information after it has been buried, or one is really taking direction from the Archangel Smearel, rather than stand up and plead guilty to originating a communication. Unless one can originate communications one's imagination is in bad shape. The reverse does not happen to be true. The imagination is not that thing which is first imperiled and then results in failure to originate communication. Failure of communication origin then results in failure of imagination, so the rehabilitation of communication origin rehabilitates as well the imagination.

This is very good news, indeed, for anyone in the creative arts particularly, but who is not in the creative arts?

In examining the whole subject of communication, one discovers that there are very few people around him in this day and age who are actually communicating, and there are a lot of people who think they are communicating who are not.

The AMA would like to believe that I am in the latter category.

11

Pan-Determinism

11

Pan-Determinism

An entirely new concept in Dianetics and Scientology is that of pan-determinism.

In Book One we talked about self-determinism. Self-determinism meant, in essence, control by the awareness of awareness unit of that which it conceived to be its identity. Some effort in Book One was made to move self-determinism out into the remaining dynamics.

Pan-determinism is a word which describes determinism all along the dynamics. Actually, self-determinism attempted to do this, and our earlier idea of self-determinism was a sort of pan-determinism.

We have to remember here that the dynamics involved in Dianetics are the first four. The dynamics involved in Scientology are the last four of the total set of eight. The eight dynamics are as follows:

Dynamic one is the urge toward survival as self.

Dynamic two is the urge toward survival through sex or children, and embraces both the sexual act and the care and raising of children.

Dynamic three is the urge toward survival through the group and as the group.

Dynamic four is the urge toward survival through all mankind and as all mankind.

Dynamic five is the urge toward survival through life forms such as animals, birds, insects, fish and vegetation, and is the urge to survive as these.

Dynamic six is the urge toward survival through the physical universe and has as its components matter, energy, space and time, from which we derive the word MEST.

Dynamic seven is the urge toward survival through spirit and would include the manifestations or the totality of awareness of awareness units, thetans, demons, ghosts, spirits, godlings, and so forth.

Dynamic eight is the urge toward survival through the Supreme Being or, more exactly, infinity. It is called dynamic eight because it is infinity turned up on its side.

The urge toward survival through self, sex, children, groups and mankind is the proper province of Dianetics.

Now let us examine this concept of pan-determinism. Pan-determinism would be the willingness to determine or control self and dynamics other than self, up to the eight listed above. Like self-determinism, pan-determinism is self-elected or self-determined, in that one does it knowingly and directly, not from obsession, compulsion or inhibition. An undetermined individual, of course, does not exist, but an other-determined individual definitely can exist. Where we have self-determinism, and we interpret self-determinism as determinism on the first dynamic, we have only willingness to control self and no willingness to control anything beyond self. If this is the case, in self-determinism we have as other-determinism sex, children, groups, mankind, and going on into Scientology, animal life, vegetation, the physical universe, spirits and God—or whatever else might compose infinity.

In view of the fact that self-determinism was interpreted in this fashion it left an individual in the state of mind of being willing to be determined on all other dynamics and by all other dynamics except his own personal dynamic. In view of the fact that a personal dynamic cannot exist, and in view of the fact that all auditing is the third dynamic, and that an individual as we see him, a man, is actually a composite and is not a first dynamic but a third dynamic, we see we are in difficulties with this definition of self-determinism and continued use of self-determinism. It is necessary, then, to investigate further and to assign more precision to this concept of willingness to control.

When we say control we do not mean the "control case" where control is obsessive or other-determined, or where the individual is controlling things out of compulsion or fear. We simply mean willingness to start, stop and change. The anatomy of control is just that—starting, stopping and changing things. Now, it is not necessary for a person to start, stop and change things just to demonstrate that he can control them. He must, however, to be healthy and capable, be able to start, stop and change things.

Here we come immediately to what we mean by ability. It would be the ability to start, change and stop things, and if we have an ability to start, stop and change things, we of course must have a willingness to start, stop and change things. Those people who are unwillingly behaving in some direction so as to start, stop and change things are very sick people, and in this last category we discover the bulk of the human race at this writing.

The basic difference between aberration and sanity, between inability and ability, between illness and health, is the knowingness of causation by self opposed to unknown causation by others or other things. An individual who knows he is doing it is far more capable than one who is doing it but supposes something else is doing it. Psychosis is itself simply an inversion of determinism. A psychotic is entirely other-determined, a sane man is in good measure self-determined. Pan-determinism would mean a willingness to start, change and stop on any and all dynamics. That is its primary definition. A further definition, also a precision definition, is: the willingness to start, change and stop two or more forces, whether or not opposed; and this could be interpreted as two or more individuals, two or more groups, two or more planets, two or more life species, two or more universes, two or more spirits, whether or not opposed. This means that one would not necessarily fight, he would not necessarily choose sides.

This is in total controversy to some of the most cherished beliefs of man, but may I point out to you quickly that man is not an entirely sane person, and thus some of his beliefs must be somewhat aberrated. There is such a thing as courage, but there is not such a thing as sanity totally opposed.

People who are afraid of control are liable to be afraid of pan-determinism, but if they will see this as a willingness to start, change and stop any dynamic they will see that a person must be assuming the responsibility for any of the dynamics. A conqueror, in his onslaught[1] against society, is fighting other-determinisms. He is starting, changing and stopping things

---

1. **onslaught:** a violent, intense attack.

because of an unwillingness to associate with or support other races or customs than his own. Therefore, what he is doing can be interpreted as bad.

In support of this we get all of the earlier religious teachings, but these have been grossly misinterpreted. These have been interpreted to mean that a person should not fight in any way, or defend anything, or have anything, or own anything. This is not true. A person who is willing to be other identities besides himself, other individualities besides himself, does not necessarily harm these other individualities. Indeed, we cannot make the complete distinction of other than himself, since we are saying in this that he clings to something he calls self and supports and defends it without being willing to identify himself with others.

One of the most maddening debaters is one who moves at will between the viewpoints of himself and those who have elected him as an enemy.

There is an important scale down from pan-determinism. It does not lead along a dwindling dynamic path, but it could, of course. One could simply see his pan-determinism dwindling, the falling off of one dynamic after another, until one is down to first dynamic, but that is not a particularly workable picture and an auditor does not use it.

The scale down from pan-determinism is Pan-determinism, Fighting, Must and Must not happen again, Repair and association. These are actually processes. At the bottom we find an unwillingness to associate with anything. Just above this is an unwillingness to repair anything, but a willingness to associate somewhat. Above this is a willingness to associate and to repair somewhat, but no willingness to let certain things happen again. Above this is a willingness to fight things, and above this is pan-determinism. These are arranged in this fashion because this is the ladder a preclear climbs if he is run on a certain type of process. This is something like the old emotional scale, which went apathy, grief, fear, anger, antagonism, boredom, conservatism, and enthusiasm, only in this case it is a scale of behavior manifestations. Where an individual who is unwilling to associate with various things is certainly a long way from being pan-determined and definitely is not even self-determined, he has to come up a ways before he is willing to repair anything, but in this frame of mind he can repair quite generally, but is unwilling or unable to create or destroy. An oddity here is that a person who is unwilling to associate is only able to destroy, and a person has to be very far up this scale before he can create. In fact, he has to be up around pan-determinism to adequately create. Above this level of repair we find an individual frozen in many incidents which he is preventing from occurring once more and is holding the facsimiles or engrams of these incidents so that he will have a model and so know what mustn't occur; and above this level we discover an individual fighting or being willing to fight almost anything; and above this level we discover an individual willing or able to be almost anything and so may be at peace with things and does not have to fight things. An individual at a pan-determinism level can create. An individual at Association, as I have said, can only destroy. An individual at Repair and Must and Must not happen again is making a very heavy effort—and I do mean effort—to survive.

Let us take for our example of pan-determinism the second dynamic. Here we find such a thorough effort to have other-determinism that Freud picked this out as the only aberrative factor. It is not the only aberrative factor, but in view of the fact that it is a desired inflow it can be considered, with many other things, to have some aberrative value. Let us look at it from terms of self-determinism and pan-determinism. Here we have an individual believing himself to be a man, who believes that his only sexual pleasure can be derived from remaining very solidly a man and having sexual relationships with a woman, and being very sure that he is not the woman. On the other hand, we find the woman determined to be herself and experience as herself, and to experience a sexual inflow from a man. In the case of the man, as in the case of the woman, we have an unwillingness to be the other sex. This is considered natural, but do you know that when this is entirely true, when we have complete determinism to be self and not to be to any slightest degree the other person, there is no sexual pleasure interchange of any kind whatsoever? We get the condition known as satyrism[2] and nymphomania.[3] We get a tremendous anxiety to have a sexual flow.

Probably the only reason you can see the universe at all is because you are still willing to be some part of it. Probably the only reason you can talk to people is because you can also be the other person you are talking to. Probably the only reason you can really let people talk to you is because you are willing to let the other person be you, somewhat, and he is willing to let you be him to some degree. In view of the fact that space itself is a mock-up, is a state of mind, it can be seen that individuality depends to some degree upon the law that no two things must occupy the same space. When we get this law in action we have a universe. Until this law goes into action there is no universe, and one would be hard put to differentiate entirely. Two things can occupy the same space to the degree that you are willing to believe they can. It is a very easy thing to talk to an audience if you are perfectly willing to be an audience. It is a very difficult thing to talk to an audience if you are unwilling to be an audience. Similarly, it is very difficult to be an audience if you are unwilling to be on the stage. One could conceive that a person

---

2. **satyrism:** state or condition of uncontrollable sexual desire in men.

3. **nymphomania:** abnormal and uncontrollable desire by a woman for sexual intercourse.

who had a considerable amount of stage fright would be incapable of enjoying the performance of actors. And so it is. We discover the person who is in the audience and has, himself, considerable stage fright—writhing and feeling embarrassed for every actor who makes the slightest slip or mistake. In other words, we find this person compulsively being on the stage although he is in the audience.

Things of this nature have led more than one philosopher to assume that we were all from the same mold, or that we were all the same thing. This is a very moot[4] question. Processing demonstrates rather adequately that we are all really individuals and that we are not the same individual, and indeed, people who believe we are all the same individual have a very rough time of it. But evidently we could all be the same individual, at least if we were entirely sane.

The physical universe is a sort of a hypnotic trance where the individual believes himself to be capable of viewing from various points. The illusion is rendered very excellent by the fact that other individuals believe that they are viewing the same things from the same points as they occupy. We are all, as awareness of awareness units, basically different. We are not the same "pool of life," and we are all evidently differently endowed, no matter what the Communist Party would like to believe.

One of the most significant differences from man to man is the degree to which he is willing to be pan-determined. The man who has to forcefully control everything in his vicinity, including his family, is not being self-determined, usually, much less pandetermined. He is not being his family. If he were being his family, he would understand why they were doing what they were doing and he would not feel that there was any danger or

---

4. **moot:** so hypothetical as to be meaningless.

menace in their going on executing the motions or emanating the emotions which they do. But, anchored down as one person, rather obsessed with the damage that can be done to him or those around him, an individual is apt to launch himself upon a course of heavy, solid, super-control of others. Now let us take the person who is self-determined and pan-determined in the same situation, and we discover that he would have enough understanding in the vicinity of his family, and of his family, and with this understanding would be willing to be and experience as the remainder of the family, and we would find out that he actually could control the family with considerable ease. The oddity of it is that force can only control down into entheta—to enturbulation—but that a pan-determinism controls upward into greater happiness and understanding since there is more ARC present. You have seen individuals around whom a great deal of peace and quiet obtained. Such individuals quite commonly hold into sanity and cheerfulness many others in their environment who are not basically stable or self-determined at all. The individual who is doing this is not doing it out of obsession, he is doing it simply by knowing and being. He understands what people are talking about because he is perfectly willing to be these people. When he falls away from understanding what they are talking about he has also fallen away from being willing to be them. Willingness to understand and willingness to be are, for our purposes, synonymous.

Now how does this pan-determinism tie into communication?

We have seen that difficulties arise on the cycle of communication and on the two-way cycle of communication when origins of communication, answers and acknowledgments were scarce. This must be, then, that the individual, becoming aberrated through communication, must have conceived the necessity of another determinism. In other words, one has to fall away from pan-determinism to get into any of the traps of communication at all.

It is a very fortunate thing for us that pan-determinism exists, otherwise there would be absolutely no way whatsoever out of this maze of miscommunications that a person gets into. The only way out of it would be to have other people come around and do enough talking and go to enough movies, and seek out another self-determinism which would communicate and make it communicate until one was sane. However, it doesn't happen to work out in an unlimited sense in this way. The oddity is that it works out in "mock-up." Further, it works out best in mock-up, for in mock-up we introduce the idea of pan-determinism.

When we ask somebody to get the idea that somebody else is present, who is not, and then have him make this person give him answers, we discover after a while that some major aberrations have blown out of our preclear. In the first part the preclear is actually remedying the scarcity of answers—or, if these were being processed, origins or acknowledgments—and is so disentangling communication lines. The sense of what he would mock the person up as saying would have nothing to do with it. The communication could be almost pure gibberish as long as it was an answer. This would straighten out the bank to a very marked degree. The other factor which enters into this is pan-determinism. We are making the individual actually mock up somebody else and make somebody else say something. In other words, we are making our preclear take over the control, the start, change and stop of another communication medium. And with further test and experiment we discover that we can do this for all the dynamics, and when we have done it for all the dynamics we have brought our preclear up to a point of where he is willing to monitor communications on all the dynamics. And when he is willing to do this, and get origins, answers and acknowledgments along all the dynamics, we find that we have a very serene person who can do the most remarkable things. Anything you have read about concerning the potential abilities of the Clear, and a lot more, comes true when we follow this course. So it is a very fortunate thing for us that pan-determinism exists. Otherwise there would be no processing anybody.

Remember, when you are explaining this to people, that it is *willingness* to control on any and all dynamics, and that it is not obsessive or compulsive control to own, protect or hide on any dynamic. All the ills of Earth come from an obsession to own, control, protect and hide on other dynamics than self. The true enlightenments of this world have come from willingness to *be* along any of the dynamics.

One of the things which gives truth to pan-determinism is the savageness with which the aberrated attempt to drive an individual away from anything resembling pan-determinism. This is simply an obsessive action on the part of people to climb up to pan-determinism by force. Pan-determinism cannot be climbed by force. The ladder to that height is not made of pikes and spears, spankings and police forces. It is made of understanding—affinity, reality and communication.

12

The Six Basic Processes

12

The Six
Basic Processes

Today's auditor must be conversant with six basic processes and must be able to get results with these processes before he can expect to get results with higher levels of auditing.

These six processes form a roadway for more than the auditor. We discover that they compose a Tone Scale. This Tone Scale is as follows: at its lowest and highest reaches, whether by mimicry, words or mock-up, we have Two-way Communication. Next above this, occupying the position from about 1.1 to 1.8 on the Chart of Human Evaluation[1] as given in *Science of Survival*, we have Elementary Straightwire.[2] Above this we have, from 1.8 to 2.5, Opening Procedure of 8-C. Above this, from 2.6 to 3.0, we have Opening Procedure by Duplication. Above this we have Remedy of Havingness, from 3.1 to 3.5, and above this, from 3.6 to 4.0, Spotting Spots in Space.[3]

---

1. **Chart of Human Evaluation:** a chart organized in very early 1951 by L. Ron Hubbard. It has various columns and gives behavior characteristics. It is plotted out mathematically on the basis of ARC; a very good chart to use in order to predict people. (For further information on this chart, read Ron's book *Science of Survival*.)

2. **Elementary Straightwire:** a basic process with two commands: "Give me something you wouldn't mind remembering," "Give me something you wouldn't mind forgetting."

3. **Spotting Spots in Space:** a process in which the goal is to bring the preclear to a point where he can spot locations in space which do not have color, mass or shape but which are simply locations, and spot that same location repeatedly without variation.

Chart of Processes
Where they are on the ARC Scale

Exteriorized	
Spot Spots in Space	4.0
Spot Spots in Space	3.6
Remedy of Havingness	3.5
Remedy of Havingness	3.1
Opening Procedure by Duplication	3.0
Opening Procedure by Duplication	2.6
Opening Procedure of 8-C	2.5
Opening Procedure of 8-C	1.8
Elementary Straightwire	1.8
Elementary Straightwire	1.1
Two-way Communication	1.0
Two-way Communication	-8.0
"One-Shot Clear"	4.0
"One-Shot Clear"	2.5

An auditor, in auditing these six basic processes, becomes sufficiently capable in observing and communicating that he can handle (or can bring a preclear up to the point where he can handle) the "subjective process" which remedies communication, or the other one which is the "One-Shot Clear."

The problem of psychosis never rightly belonged in Dianetics, but it has been solved there. Opening Procedure of 8-C and the mimicry techniques as given in the PABs[4] resolve psychosis. They resolve it rapidly and care for it adequately, and we have no real worry on that score. The only reason we would

---

4. **PABs:** Professional Auditor's Bulletins. These are issues written by L. Ron Hubbard between 10 May 1953 and 15 May 1959. The content of these bulletins are technical and promotional. Their intent is to give the professional auditor and his preclears the best possible processes and processing available at the moment it becomes available.

enter the field of psychosis at all would be to find out how far south[5] our techniques worked. These six basic processes also resolve psychosomatic illness and do other remarkable things.

As covered much more fully in *The Creation of Human Ability*, these six basic processes form the background to all processes. Through them we find two-way communication everywhere. It can be said with honesty that there is no auditing without two-way communication.

The process, Two-way Communication itself, could be subdivided into verbal and non verbal processes. The verbal processes would include questions about the present-time environment and the preclear's life, interests, and so forth, and would get a direct answer to every question, no matter how long the communication lag was. In other words, a two-way communication would be entered upon so as to actually bring the preclear to talk to the auditor. In the case of people who have great difficulties in this line, we have nonverbal techniques such as Mimicry, wherein the auditor mimics the preclear and persuades the preclear to mimic the auditor. Various processes are used, such as passing a ball back and forth between them, nodding, shaking hands, sitting down, standing up and walking across the room and back and sitting down, all of which are effective.

Much of this book, *Dianetics 55!* is on the subject of two-way communication, and the totality of auditing is bringing a preclear into excellent two-way communication, and it is conceived a little difficult by instructors to relay the "process" called Two-way Communication. However, it is actually simplicity itself, for all that is necessary is to get the preclear to actually

---

5. **south:** out the bottom, losing, etc.

volunteer communications and answer the communications volunteered to him. There is always something the preclear will talk about.

Mimicry, particularly when used on psychotics, is a precision subject. Mimicry is not a new process, it is almost as old as psychotherapy, but it is spotty when used without an intimate knowledge of validation. It can be said that, that which one validates comes true. The only force or strength life has is that which derives directly from the upper echelon of understanding. When life gets down to a point where it is incomprehensible, it cannot relay any understanding. Understanding this is essential for an auditor. He must realize that he gives power to everything he validates. We made something important out of the engram, and by validating engrams, we actually, where they were audited poorly, gave force and power to engrams. Thus it is with the psychotic. To mimic the strange, peculiar, bizarre and unusual things he does is to give force and strength to those things. It cannot be said with sufficient emphasis that the auditor must *never* mimic the strange, bizarre and unusual manifestations of the psychotic. The only way that the auditor can make mimicry work consistently and continually and rapidly, is by validating what the environment considers the agreed-upon, the usual, the routine, the ordinary. Perhaps a psychotic is twisting his hands madly, and occasionally nodding slightly. The auditor, in mimicking him, would *not* twist his hands, but would nod slightly, since a nod is the agreed-upon manifestation in the environment, not the twisting of hands. If the auditor does this, the preclear will begin to nod more and twist his hands less. If the auditor were to begin to mimic the psychotic by twisting hands, he would discover that the psychotic would probably stop twisting his hands, but would do something else much more bizarre. And if the auditor then mimicked this much more bizarre thing, the psychotic would simply go on to something even wilder or might become entirely motionless, for the one fear the psychotic has is becoming predictable. The psychotic is under the control of entities, demon circuits. He does have a grain of sanity present, otherwise he would not be able to function at all. Therefore, those things which he does which are sane must be mimicked and so reinforced. If an auditor knows this thoroughly and practices it smartly he will discover that psychotics can be brought into two-way communication and moved immediately into Opening Procedure of 8-C, the proper process for psychotics. 8-C, while not a psychotic process, does work on psychotics. However, in working Opening Procedure of 8-C on the psychotic, the auditor must be very careful not to go beyond part "a" for a long, long time.

From the process known as "Two-way Communication" we move on to the process known as "Elementary Straightwire." Elementary Straightwire has two basic commands. One of these commands is used continually, over and over and over and over, until the communication lag is entirely flat on it. Then the other command is used over and over and over until the communication lag is entirely flat, at which time it will be discovered that the first command will now give communication lags. And so it is used over and over and over and then the second one is used over and over and over. In other words, what we do here is to use this process of Elementary Straightwire with just two commands, continuingly, one command at a time, flattening each communication lag encountered. While doing this, of course, one maintains a two-way communication. He acknowledges the fact that the preclear has recalled something and is in general alert to receive from the preclear an originated communication, answer it, and give further orders. The two commands of Elementary Straightwire are

"Give me something you wouldn't mind remembering,"

"Give me something you wouldn't mind forgetting."

This can be varied with:

"Tell me something you wouldn't mind remembering,"

"Tell me something you wouldn't mind forgetting."

This Elementary Straightwire is a standard form. If it is varied it should be varied toward simplicity. A simple form of Straightwire is "Remember something," over and over, again and again and again and again and again. Do not use, however, "Forget something," since this is far too rough for the preclear. Another even simpler form is to apply "Remember something" to the dynamics, such as "Remember a man," "Remember a group." The only error that can be made in Elementary Straightwire is to get too fancy, for one does not believe that an auditor who has advanced this far in auditing would make an error in communication. There is an entire gamut[6] which we call "The next to the last list in *Self Analysis*" published in the original edition of *Self Analysis* which has many times been known to break a person from a neurotic to a sane state. This is

"Can you recall a time that is really real to you?"

"Can you recall a time when you were communicating well to someone?"

"Can you recall a time when someone was communicating well to you?"

"Can you recall a time when you felt affinity for someone?"

"Can you recall a time when someone felt affinity for you?"

By keeping this in the understanding or affinity line a case advances more rapidly than if misemotion and other factors are addressed.

---

6. **gamut:** the entire range or extent of something.

Opening Procedure of 8-C is one of the most effective and powerful processes ever developed and should be recognized and used as such. The main error which is made with the Opening Procedure of 8-C is not to do it long enough. It takes about fifteen hours of Opening Procedure of 8-C in order to bring a person into a completely relaxed and self-determined state of mind regarding orders. Opening Procedure of 8-C is a precision process. Step "a" of Opening Procedure of 8-C is:

"Do you see that object?" the auditor pointing.

When the preclear signifies that he does, the auditor says, "Walk over to it."

When the preclear has walked over to it, the auditor says, "Touch it."

When the preclear does, the auditor says, "Let go,"

and designates another object—a wall, a lamp—calls them by name or not, and goes through the same procedure once more. It is important that the auditor specifically acknowledge each time the preclear has executed the command given. When the preclear has seen the object, when he has walked over to it, when he has touched it, when he has let it go—each time, the auditor signifies that he has perceived and does acknowledge this action on the part of the preclear. This Step "a" is used until the preclear does it easily, smoothly, without the slightest variation or introduction of any physical communication lag, and has demonstrated completely that he has no upset feeling about the auditor or objects in the room.

When "a" has been run for a length of time necessary to bring the case uptone, Part "b" is run. Part "b" introduces the idea of decision. It is notable that the "One-Shot Clear" must be very strong on this power of decision. It is also notable that a person in extremely bad condition has no power of decision. The commands of Part "b" are:

"Pick a spot in this room."

and when the preclear has, "Walk over to it,"

and when the preclear does, "Put your finger on it,"

and when the preclear has, "Let go."

Each time, the auditor acknowledges the completion of the command by the preclear, signifying "All right" or "Okay," or "Fine," making it very plain that he has noticed and approves of and is acknowledging the action of the preclear in following each specific command. He approves of these one at a time in this fashion. The preclear is run on this until he demonstrates no physical communication lag of any kind in making up his mind what to touch, how to touch it, and so forth.

Part "c" of Opening Procedure of 8-C introduces further decision. It goes as follows:

The auditor says, "Pick a spot in this room,"

and when the preclear has, the auditor says, "Walk over to it."

When the preclear does, the auditor says, "Make up your mind when you are going to place your finger on it, and do so."

When the preclear has done this, the auditor says, "Make up your mind when you are going to let go, and let go."

The auditor each time acknowledges the completion of one of these orders to the preclear.

In doing Opening Procedure of 8-C the preclear must not be

permitted to execute a command before it is given, and a two-way communication must be maintained. As I have said, Opening Procedure of 8-C is a very powerful process. If all auditors knew how to do was Opening Procedure of 8-C and could do this very well, we would right there have psychotherapy licked. But we are not trying to lick psychotherapy. It has never been a major problem to us. We are trying to bring people a long way further north[7] than psychotherapy ever dreamed of, and Dianetics and Scientology are not psychotherapies, they are processes which increase the abilities of people.

Opening Procedure by Duplication has as its goal the separating of time, moment from moment. This is done by getting a preclear to duplicate his same action over and over again with two dissimilar objects. In England this process is called "Book and Bottle," probably because these two familiar objects are the most used in doing Opening Procedure by Duplication.

The first step of Opening Procedure by Duplication is to familiarize the preclear with both objects, as to their reality and his ability to own them. One makes him handle them, and feel them, and acquaint himself with them, makes him describe them as objects he is experiencing in present time, not as something related into the past. A little time spent on this can be quite beneficial.

The auditor then begins what will become to the preclear, before he is through with this, some of the most hated phrases anyone could conceive, but which, by the time the preclear is finished with this, become just like any other phrases. Many people believe that Opening Procedure by Duplication induces hypnosis. This is because in running it hypnotism runs off. The preclear, while the hypnotism is running off, may feel quite

---

7. **north:** in the direction of case improvement.

hypnotized. It is the exact reverse of hypnotism. Hypnotism is an effort to persuade the individual to do nothing, to sit still, and to accept fully the inflow. Opening Procedure by Duplication contains two-way communication, and indeed does not work unless two-way communication is done with it. The main liability in doing two-way communication on Opening Procedure by Duplication is that the auditor, in introducing two-way communication to it, may stray considerably from the pattern laid down. He must not do this. Although he is maintaining two-way communication he must adhere very sharply to the process. He can make the preclear tell more about them; he can make the preclear describe various things which are manifesting themselves to the preclear; he can be insistent the preclear really knows he has just picked this up; but he must stay with this sequence of auditing commands, and may not vary from them even vaguely. He can interject other conversation, but not other auditing commands, into Opening Procedure by Duplication.

The auditing commands are

"Do you see that book?" says the auditor, pointing.

When the preclear signifies that he has, the auditor says, "Walk over to it."

When the preclear does, the auditor says, "Pick it up."

When the preclear does, the auditor says, "Look at it."

When the preclear does (usually he was looking at it but now looks at it more closely) the auditor says, "Give me its color."

When the preclear does, the auditor says, "Give me its weight."

When the preclear does, the auditor says, "Give me its temperature."

When the preclear has, the auditor says, "Put it back exactly as you found it."

This action sequence having been completed, the auditor points to the bottle. "Do you see that bottle?"

When the preclear does, the auditor says, "Walk over to it."

When the preclear does, the auditor says, "Pick it up."

When the preclear has, the auditor says, "Look at it."

When the preclear does, the auditor says, "Give me its color."

When the preclear has, the auditor says, "Give me its weight."

When the preclear has, the auditor says, "Give me its temperature."

When the preclear has, the auditor says, "Put it back exactly as you found it."

Then the auditor says, pointing at the book, "Do you see that book?" and so on, back and forth, using this exact sequence of commands.

The auditor can interject "Describe it more fully."

The auditor can sometimes, but not more often than once every fifteen minutes, point to the book, have the preclear go through the full sequence with the book, and then point to the book again, and have the preclear once more go through the full sequence with the book. This will break down the automatic machinery a preclear is bound to set up to compensate for this process. We want to keep the preclear doing it, not his machines. By asking the preclear to describe the object, or describe its temperature more fully in its proper sequence in these commands, machines are also broken down and the alertness and awareness of the preclear is increased.

The auditor must not omit letting the preclear give him the preclear's reactions. The preclear will pause, seem to be confused. It is up to the auditor at that moment to say, "What happened?" and to find out what happened, and then to continue with the process, having acknowledged the communication of the preclear. An auditor must never be afraid to let a preclear emanate a communication, and an auditor must never fail to acknowledge the completion of an auditing action, no matter how minute.

The Remedy of Havingness is an extremely effective process for it remedies the ability of the preclear to have or not have at will. Sometimes auditors interpret this process as inflow, only. That is because the physical universe is an inflow universe, and it is all too easy for an auditor to assign to auditing, and all other actions, inflow characteristics only.

The modus operandi of the Remedy of Havingness is to have the preclear mock up something, pull it in, or mock up something and throw it away. It does not matter what you have him mock up. The item can have significance or not as the case may be. Preclears who are low in tone, if this is run on them— and it should not be—have a tendency to make everything they mock up very significant. It is not the significance, it is the mass which counts. However, to keep the preclear interested, or to assist his mocking up, an auditor may designate specific things, and does so.

It will be found that the acceptance level and expectance level of the preclear very definitely monitor what he mocks up, and what he can pull in and what he can throw away. As covered in the Professional Auditor's Bulletins, Acceptance Level Processes[8] can be combined with Remedy of Havingness.

The commands of Remedy of Havingness are as follows:

"Mock up a (planet, man, brick)."

"Make a copy of it."

"Make a copy of it."

"Make a copy of it."

And when the preclear has from five to fifteen copies, "Push them all together."

"Now pull them in on you."

When the preclear has done this for some time, the last command is varied by saying, "Throw them away and have them disappear in the distance."

In other words, we have the preclear mock up something; when he has we have him make a copy of it, make another copy and another copy and another copy, one at a time, push them together and pull them in or throw them away. We keep up this process for some time until we are very certain that he can actually throw things away or pull them in on himself at will. This is the Remedy of Havingness. Remedy of Havingness does not mean stuffing the preclear with energy. It means remedying his ability to have or not have energy. Run with particular

---

8. **Acceptance Level Processes:** the five stages of Acceptance Level Processing. One has the preclear mock up, no matter how blackly or how crudely, items for himself to accept; then have others in his mock-ups mock up things for them to accept, and others to mock up things for others to accept. This extends to having the preclear also mock up things for others to accept and others to mock up things for the preclear to accept.

significances such as money, women, etc., one could remedy specific scarcities on the part of the preclear. But remember, they may be so scarce that at first he will have to waste a large quantity of them before he can have one.

On an awareness of awareness unit exteriorized we run Remedy of Havingness a little differently. We say, "Put up eight anchor points.[9]" We describe to him how we want these put up. We want them put up in such a way as to form the corners of a cube. In other words, these eight anchor points are not to be in a group in front or behind the preclear, but they are to be distributed around him. When the preclear has done this we say, "Pull them into you." We keep this up for a long time. We also have the preclear exteriorized mock up eight anchor points and send them away from him. A preclear exteriorized can be very unhappy about his lack of havingness and this last process is used to remedy this upset.

Remedy of Havingness is an exteriorization technique. If it is run on an individual long enough, say eight or ten hours, he will probably exteriorize at the end of that time. If you kept on running it as an exteriorized process, given in the second part above, he would then have his visio[10] clear up, and he would finally get into very excellent condition. This is quite a process. However, remember this process depends upon the preclear following the auditor's orders. Unless the auditor has guaranteed this by Opening Procedure of 8-C and Opening Procedure by Duplication, the chances of the preclear actually following his orders (although pretending to do so) are very slim. We have discovered in old-time Dianetics that the breakdown was in the

---

9. **anchor points:** points which demark the outermost boundaries of a space or its corners.

10. **visio:** the recall of something seen, so that it is seen again in the mind in full color, scale, dimension, brightness and detail.

failure of the preclear to follow the auditor's orders. Preclears would pretend to follow an auditor's orders but actually would not.

The process known as Spotting Spots in Space is not to be attempted on somebody who is having a difficult time, and, when it is attempted, it should be accompanied with Remedy of Havingness. One makes a person spot spots in space for a short time, then remedy havingness, then spot spots in space, then remedy havingness, then spot spots in space. These two processes, Remedy of Havingness, Spotting Spots in Space actually belong together, however the preclear eventually emerges up into a higher band where he can spot spots in space without remedying his havingness.

The auditing commands are

"Spot a spot in the space of this room."

When the preclear has, the auditor says, "Spot another spot," etc.

When the preclear gets well into the process in this fashion we say, "Spot a spot in the space of this room."

"Walk over to it."

When he has, "Put your finger on it."

When he does, "Let go."

The auditor should ask a preclear when he starts this process if the spot has any mass, color, temperature or any other characteristic, or "How big is it?" The auditor asks this to make sure this preclear is actually spotting a spot, a simple location, not a spot that has mass or temperature or characteristics. A location is simply a location. It does not have mass; it does not have color; it does not have temperature. When we ask the preclear to spot a spot at first his spots are liable to have mass and temperature. We do not object to this, we simply ask him frequently, once we have discovered that his spots do have this, how his spots are getting along, and we remember, on such a preclear, that we must remedy havingness. Eventually he will move out to a point where he is simply spotting locations.

These are the six basic processes that an auditor must know. They are all of them very powerful processes, and each and any one of them can accomplish the goals which were envisioned in *Dianetics: The Modern Science of Mental Health.* The essence of these processes is to do them as given, to do them "purely," all the while maintaining a two-way communication with the preclear. Auditors get into minor variations on this set of processes, but these processes were evolved first from theory by myself, were developed in practice by myself, and were then given to many auditors to do, and many auditors were trained in them, and then these processes were refined and inspected, and refined and inspected until they represent a very broad agreement. And we have found that these commands, as you have them here, are the best commands which can be used in processing a preclear. The failure of an auditor to duplicate, his unwillingness to duplicate, his upset about duplication in general will quite often lead him up the blind alley of varying a process compulsively or obsessively. When he does he can expect to lessen the results. Auditing today, by the experience of a very large number of auditors, is a very severe discipline on the individual. It is not an art, and it never will be an art. It is a precision science. In the old days, all this talk about art and intuition and instinctiveness cost a lot of preclears the benefit of auditing. Auditing in the long ago was tremendously complicated, but it was nonetheless precise. Now that it is very simple, it is still very precise.

Among these processes an understanding of communication lag and Opening Procedure of 8-C were chosen as the two processes to be taught to a very large area which contained a large number of auditors. This area had been noteworthy, heretofore, for the strange results "obtained" by auditors and the strange techniques which were used in it. A couple of auditors were sent into this area to teach everybody communication lag and Opening Procedure of 8-C. Actually these two auditors were originally from this area. They did so, and several lives have been reported saved to date, and a great many cases have been salvaged, and the entire science is looking up in that particular area simply because the area was taught nothing but communication lag and the Opening Procedure of 8-C and did nothing thereafter but this. Out in the outskirts of this area a couple of auditors varied Opening Procedure by Duplication and were reported to be having very good luck with the variation, but these two auditors were not part of the crew who were taught Opening Procedure of 8-C and communication lag, and the results they are obtaining are very junior to the results being obtained by their own fellows very close by.

It could be said that the only real danger in auditing was failure. Auditing is the start, change and stop of aberration, or the creation of ability. Today creation of ability takes prominence to a point where aberration drops out of sight and is forgotten. But the auditor who does not obtain results is demonstrating to himself that he cannot control human aberration and human ability, and the demonstration of his failure to himself is sufficient to make him slightly incapable in handling his own difficulties. Thus, it is a tremendously important thing that we have processes which, when used exactly as given, and used with skill, produce uniformly good results on preclears. An auditor using these on preclears gets better and better and better and better even when he doesn't have any auditing himself—a thing which was not the story of 1950. When you can control aberration in others, when you can increase the ability of others, you certainly do not worry about your own. An auditor who has consistent failures will eventually drop back to self-auditing, but these processes will cure even that. Self-auditing, of course, is the manifestation of going around running concepts or processes on one's self. One is doing this because he has been made afraid, through his failure on others, of his ability to control his own engrams, facsimiles, thoughts and concepts, and he seeks to control them through auditing. It is not necessary for an individual to audit himself in order to control his own machinery.

Before anyone should adventure in the direction of testing the "One-Shot Clear" or doing anything about exteriorizing the awareness of awareness unit and so making a Clear, he should be entirely conversant with these processes. Actually, any of these processes run long enough would probably result in an exteriorization. There are faster ways to achieve an exteriorization than these processes, but these processes are preliminary to them. The preclear who cannot follow the auditor's orders will not sit there and do a subjective—which is to say, an out-of-sight, in his own mind—process without varying it. The trouble with the preclear is that he cannot duplicate, he cannot follow the orders of the auditor, and when the auditor tells him to run a concept or a thought, the preclear probably pays token nod to this and runs entirely something else. A very close E-Meter review of a number of preclears who were not advancing under "subjective processes" disclosed that each and every one of them had never run what the auditor told them to run. They were afraid of obeying the auditor, they were afraid of what the auditor was doing, they were afraid of his skill. Opening Procedure of 8-C remedies this fear and brings the inability and unwillingness of the preclear out into the open where it belongs.

In Opening Procedure by Duplication we very often get a preclear "blowing the session" where the auditor has run an insufficient quantity of Opening Procedure of 8-C. When a preclear "blows a session" on Opening Procedure by Duplication, the auditor has missed. He has not run enough Opening

Procedure of 8-C. How much is enough Opening Procedure of 8-C? Until the person is in very good condition as *Homo sapiens*.

Remember that whether the command is physical or mental, the auditor must observe communication lag. In Opening Procedure of 8-C he simply repeats the process commands all the way through, and then again and again and again and in such a way flattens any lag which shows up. He does not repeat the command on which the preclear got the lag. It is easier to do this way; it is a more orderly process when it is done this way. By very close theory, the actual command on which the preclear lagged should be repeated again, but this is not done.

These are the six basic processes which we must know before we can constitute ourselves auditors today. These are the processes which are getting results. These are the processes which are making able men and able women.

These processes can be varied into specific uses where ability is concerned. One of the uses of these, for instance, would be to raise the ability of a pilot to fly a plane, or a person to drive a car, simply by having him approach, touch and let go of various parts of the object to be controlled. The exact procedure as given above of Opening Procedure is run, except that the object to be controlled is used. Typists have learned to type better, people have learned to drive cars better, and many other abilities have been recovered simply by running 8-C. One could envision a pianist who was getting tired, run-down or upset by his music, coming into full awareness of it once more simply by running 8-C on his instrument or instruments.

If we wanted to increase the ability of a salesman, it would only be necessary to run any of the above processes in their proper position on the Tone Scale to increase his ability. Abilities increase in general when these are run.

When does one run what process? One should have a copy of the Chart of Human Evaluation from *Science of Survival* and know that chart well in order to understand exactly where one starts. In general practice, however, an auditor simply starts with Two-Way Communication, and when he is getting answers to his questions and is talking rather freely with his preclear he goes into Elementary Straightwire, and from Elementary Straightwire he goes into Opening Procedure of 8-C.

There is a variation on Two-Way Communication. If you have a difficulty in getting a preclear started in two-way communication it is a very easy thing to get him talking about problems, and from problems to run this one,

"What problem could you be to yourself?"

"What problem could you be to others?"

running one and then the other each time until the preclear understood he could be an infinity of problems. Many people are so thoroughly scarce on problems that they will not let any go until they know that they can create problems for themselves. When a case is stalling, he is generally finding it very hard to give up a pet problem because he knows he can't have any more. Of course, all this is basically situated on answers. He can't have any answers so he has to have problems, then from problems he finally gets to a point where he can't even have these.

Anyone desiring to be a good auditor should follow this chapter very closely, should provide himself with a copy of *The Creation of Human Ability*, and should also procure *Science of Survival*, and study them. The best way to become an auditor is to be trained as an auditor. We have found this so much the case that while we still offer an examination to anyone who wishes to take it to the grade of Hubbard Certified Auditor,[11] or Hubbard Dianetic Auditor,[12] we never expect them to pass it—for they never have, even though it is on the most simple elements as you see before you. There is no substitute for good training.

---

11. **Hubbard Certified Auditor (HCA):** a person who has completed a course of auditor training specializing in Scientology theory and application as part of the Phoenix Certification Course in late 1954. Today, an HCA is known as a Class II auditor.

12. **Hubbard Dianetic Auditor (HDA):** a person who has completed auditor training specializing in Dianetics theory and application in the Phoenix Certification Course in late 1954. Today, an HDA is a person who completes the Hubbard Dianetics Auditor Course.

13

The Processing of Communication

13

The Processing of Communication

If you will examine the six basic processes you will discover that they are communication processes. The efficacy of 8-C derives from the fact that it places into the realm of knowingness, communication with the physical universe. The physical universe does not give us back answers, but the Opening Procedure of 8-C remedies, to a marked degree, the liability of this no-answer situation by making the individual aware of the fact that walls are simply walls, that chairs are chairs, and floors floors, and ceilings ceilings. Opening Procedure by Duplication is processing another facet of communications: Terminals, the *object* (terminal) at cause interchanging flow with the *object* (terminal) at effect. Elementary Straightwire is simply a communication with the past, and securing of answers from the past, in other words, using the *past* as a terminal. Havingness, in itself, describes the mass at a terminal, or masses, and Spotting Spots in Space improves the tolerance of an absence of a communication terminal.

These six basic processes, as designed, bring an individual up a gradient scale of tolerance for more and more communication. Once a preclear has been pressed through these he is ready for the direct processing of communication. He is not ready for the direct processing of communication until he has been put through these six basic processes.

The ability of an individual depends upon his ability to communicate. The first and foremost of mechanical abilities is this communication ability. An individual who cannot communicate with something will become the victim of that something. That which a person withdraws from in this universe becomes, to a marked degree, his master. That which one fears becomes one's master. If an individual were willing to communicate with anything and everything in the entire universe he would then be free in the entire universe. Additionally, he would have an unlimited supply of distances and terminals. A barrier, perforce, is something which an individual cannot communicate beyond. When we see space as a barrier, its total operation as a barrier is the inability of the individual to be at the other extreme end of that space or outside that space. When we see energy as a barrier, we simply see it as something which will not permit the egress[1] or ingress[2] of an individual. When we see mass, walls or time as a barrier, we mean "imagined impossibility of communication." If you do not imagine that you cannot communicate, then there cannot be a barrier.

At the same time, we are placed up against this conundrum:[3] In the absence of communication, in the absence of interchanges of communication, in the absence of other terminals, flows and terminals to which others can communicate, an awareness of awareness unit is not, by its own consideration, living. Livingness is communication. Communication is livingness. We add to this the variant degrees of affinity. We add to it agreements and obtain reality, but still these are only significances

---

1. **egress:** the act of going out or forth; emergence.
2. **ingress:** the act of entering.
3. **conundrum:** any puzzling question or problem.

entered into communication. Any and all types of significances can be entered into communication in order to "give a reason for" communication. These "reasons for" are simply reasons for a game, reasons to have communication.

In the light of the concept of pan-determinism we see that an individual has to assume that he cannot know what another is talking about if he wishes to communicate with and depend upon the communications of that other. In other words, he has to pretend that he cannot communicate. An individual, to have some sort of barrier around him, must pretend that he cannot communicate beyond that barrier. Actually, this is nothing more nor less than a pretense. These barriers are the shadows through which the fish would not move. They could have swum through these shadows except for the fact that they did not believe they could penetrate beyond the shadows. It could be said that belief alone is the reason for any entrapment.

However, there are the mechanics of entrapment and we discover that an entrapment is a communication barrier. An individual becomes entrapped in something because he does not believe he can communicate outside of it. Or he becomes fixated on a terminal *as* a terminal himself.

To be very precise, the reason why an individual is entrapped has to do with scarcity of communication. An individual is still waiting, still looking toward something, expecting it to communicate to him. It has not, and he has eventually turned his attention slightly off of this onto something else which he expects to communicate to him. And when this does not, he expects communication and so finds it elsewhere; but each time he sets up one of these expectancy lines he is to that tiny degree trapped against the terminal from which he was expecting, but did not get, a communication. Thus, we have the entire bundle known as the reactive mind, the entire anatomy of ridges, and any other enturbulative mechanism, and even problems them-selves, being a seemingly endless chain of communication scar-cities.

What are the specific scarcities in a communication line? There is no scarcity of silence. Anyone has far too much silence. Silence might be conceived to be the native state of a thetan—an awareness of awareness unit—but it is not, for obviously a thetan is alive only to the degree that he is communicating, is action—concentrated only to the degree that he is living. We discover that the tiniest cells of the body consider themselves to be the very mirrors of truth when they are the most silent. There is an interesting and peculiar test here where the auditor has the preclear mock up, in any area which contains a somatic, a great many answers or originated communications from these "dead cells" and we discover this somatic-ridden area coming to life, waking up, becoming active once more. This in itself is a specific for all types of somatics. All one has to do is have the preclear mock up answers in these dead-cell areas. An ultimate truth, which is studied to a far greater extent in *The Creation of Human Ability*, is a nothingness, but this ultimate truth is not life. Life is composed of this pretense that one cannot communicate, that one must communicate. It is composed of this intricate tangle of communications and self-erected barriers which gives us a game. When we get too deeply immersed in this game, when answers get entirely too scarce, we forget that we were the ones who interposed the idea that no answers were to be given.

Silences do not process. There is entirely too much silence on the track. Remember that. It does not process. You can fill silence, but silence itself is death. When you process silence you process the preclear down toward death, not upward toward life. The way to process him upward toward life is by supplying his scarcity of communication. We find the preclears who are in the worst condition are the preclears who are the most silent, the most out of communication. These are closest to death, closest to aberration. The way to get them alive again is to remedy some of the scarcity of communication. For a preclear who is in very poor shape, or in common practice, any preclear you encounter, you would use first the six basic steps in order to bring the individual up to something approaching a livable communication strata. And then you would go immediately into the remedy of scarcity of communication by having him mock up, himself, even if just as ideas, the various parts of the two-way cycle of communication.

The parts of the communications cycle which have to be remedied are
1. originated communications,
2. people to communicate to, or other awareness of awareness units to communicate to,
3. answers,
4. acknowledgments, and additionally, but not as important,
5. arrivals,
6. departures.

It is not necessary that the preclear have the ability to mock up or put out and hear back sound. In other words, sonic and visio are not necessary to this process. The entirety necessary is the idea of communication. You might say you have him mock up a "verbalizing idea."

The preclear will sort through, himself, parts 2, 3, 4, 5 and 6 if the preclear is simply told to "mock up some people speaking." He will, in rotation, get people answering , people acknowledging, people greeting him and people saying goodbye to him. Because the preclear is usually far down the Tone Scale on origin and ideas, and because "necessity level," other-determined forces, have been necessary to get him into communication, it is likely that he will not, himself, spot the origination of communication, and the auditor will have to call his attention to this.

Remember, this is not done on a preclear who has not first been put through his paces on the six basic processes, for an auditor sitting there asking a preclear to mock up answers or acknowledgments or originated communications could not otherwise be sure that the preclear is doing this at all. Further, the preclear's attention is very likely to stray into various portions of his own bank, for his bank starts to come to pieces under the impact of all of these communications.

The preclear must be kept at his job. His mocking up of communications must be kept in a simplicity and out of deep significances, and if his attention seems to fixate upon flows and he begins to "wrestle with mass," the auditor should get him back into mocking up communications as fast as possible.

What degree of originality is required of the preclear mocking up any of these originated communications, answers or acknowledgments? The answer to this is "none." No variety is necessary whatsoever. Simply the idea of communication, with some sort of a specific idea being communicated, is all that is necessary. Having a preclear, silent himself, mock up before him something saying "Hello," and saying "Hello" again, and saying "Hello" again, and then having him mock this up behind him saying "Hello," and saying "Hello," and saying "Hello," and saying "Hello," would be quite adequate for an originated communication. Having the preclear mock up any banality such as "All right" or "Okay," serves very well for both answers and acknowledgments. We are not at all concerned with the significance of the communication. We do not want long and involved communications. The preclear will try to get off into them. He will also try to get into his prenatal bank, his early childhood and eight lives ago. We do not want him to do this, we want him to go on mocking up originated communications, answers, acknowledgments. We are validating ability, we are not trying to get rid of inabilities in his past. We are trying to increase his ability to communicate in the present, and originate communications, and take a pan-determinism of all communicating terminals. We are not trying to get him to run out anything in the past. I know that an old Dianeticist is going to have a very hard time restraining himself from running out the prenatal which immediately appears after the preclear has made something say "Hello" to him fifteen or twenty times. It is the auditor's job today to make the preclear go on having the preclear or something say "Hello" or "Okay" or "I did it," and to ignore that engram. The number of engrams which will blow into view and beg to be run are countless. The auditor is not interested in these. Of course, if the preclear wants to tell the auditor about these, the auditor must permit the preclear to originate the communication and must answer it simply to get the preclear to originate communications. He should not let the preclear go on and on and on discussing what has occurred, once the preclear has told him the essentials of it. The auditor wants to get the preclear back onto mocking up originating communications, answers and acknowledgments. The auditor is also making the preclear mock up something to talk to while he is doing this, a point which is cared for automatically and which is not addressed actually and actively in auditing. Naturally, if there is a spot in the air out there saying "Hello" or "Okay" or "I did it," the preclear is assuming that there is something alive there that can say "Hello" to him.

All manner of thinkingness machines, large black masses, white and green fire, purple spheres, falling stars, shooting rockets, may appear in the preclear's bank while he is undergoing this process. The auditor is not interested in this phenomenon, he is merely interested in getting the preclear to mock up further communications.

It does not matter if the preclear says these communications himself aloud or simply does them quietly to himself. The necessity here is not sound. Sound is a byproduct of communication, is a carrier wave of communication and is not itself communication.

Some interesting variations can be worked on this, but they are not advised, and, indeed, they violate the terms of this process, but they demonstrate how much power this process has. One has the preclear say aloud, "Okay, Mama," a few hundred times. He will be amazed at the amount of variation which will occur, the communication lags, the impatience, the anger, the amount of data which will jump up about Mama. But this data that is jumping up is simply the bank which is triggered to agree with what the preclear is doing at this moment. In other words, that is stimulus-response. Restimulation is stimulus-response as is covered in great detail in *Dianetics: The Modern Science of Mental Health*. We could clear away an ally, we could do almost anything we wanted to do in Book One with this process of remedying the scarcity of communications.

Another point immediately arises, as to whether or not havingness has to be remedied on the preclear. It has not been found necessary to remedy havingness on the preclear if one is actually remedying the scarcity of communication. This is a great oddity, for the preclear's bank, being composed of tangled and unfinished communication lines, starts to come apart the moment that you begin to remedy the scarcity of originated communications, answers and acknowledgments. Some of these black masses which the preclear has fondly held before his face blow into forever, and yet the preclear does not need his mass remedied. The reason why he had to have mass was to compensate for the lack of communication. Where you have had a lack of communication you are liable to have a mass. As an example of this, an individual loses an ally and then keeps close by him a ring which belonged to that ally. The ring is a substitute communication terminal for the ally. After a while one begins to believe that he really has to have mass; he doesn't have to have mass at all. The remedy of the scarcity of communication cures a person of having to have mass, having to eat obsessively, or do anything else obsessively.

Along with the remedy of originated communications, the preclear's imagination rises quite markedly, and thus he is able to imagine new games and new ways of communication with sufficient rapidity to compensate for the old games which you are taking away from him. Actually the preclear, being a preclear, is a game, perhaps even the last last-ditch game in which the individual could engage.

When the auditor has the preclear run acknowledgments, the wording is "I did it." This will remedy responsibility difficulties. All automaticity comes about through lack of acknowledgments (absent players, secret players).

In view of the fact that pan-determinism is control on all dynamics, and in view of the fact that control is start, change and stop, one can have the preclear stop making things communicate for a moment, and then change the communication, and then start anew. This gives the preclear practice in starting, changing and stopping.

The auditing command which would go with this is simply:

"Mock up some answers,"

"Mock up some original communications,"

"Mock up some acknowledgments,"

with enough guiding talk to give the preclear the idea that you do not want new, startling, difficult action, but only the simple placing of communication ideas, such as "Hello," in the vicinity of the preclear over and over and over and over.

The exact auditing commands to process communications are

Originated Communications:

Auditor: "Have somebody out there, (indicating a spot in the air) start saying 'Hello' to you." The preclear does so, is himself silent. When the process is long run: Auditor: "Start saying 'Hello' to a live spot out there." The preclear aloud, or as himself, does so.

Answers:

Auditor: "Have a spot out there start saying 'Okay' to you." The preclear does this many times. Auditor: "Start saying 'Okay' to a spot out there."

Acknowledgments:

Auditor: "Have a spot out there start saying 'I did it,' " When the preclear has, many, many times: Auditor: "Start saying 'I did it' to a spot out there."

The command that turns on a somatic, repeated often enough, will turn it off.

When in doubt, remedy havingness.

This is the processing of communication directly. Remember that it is done after one has already done the six basic processes. Remember that a two-way communication is maintained with the preclear while it is being done, and remember that the preclear must be audited in full understanding and practice of the Auditor's Code, 1954. If you do this you will have Clears.

14

The
One-Shot Clear

14

The
One-Shot Clear

The goal of the "One-Shot Clear" has been with us since the earliest days of Dianetics. By "One-Shot Clear" we meant one phrase or one action given once, or repeated, which would bring into being the Clear as described in *Dianetics: The Modern Science of Mental Health*, Chapter II.

It should be understood by this time that the Clear described in *Dianetics: The Modern Science of Mental Health*, Chapter II, is actually the thetan exterior of Scientology. The way to clear somebody is to get him out of the influence of his reactive bank and his analytical machinery. When a person is so cleared, his level of knowingness is sufficient to overcome the need of machinery, and the need of stimulus-response mechanisms as contained in his reactive mind.

Long since we have had a "One-Shot Clear" for fifty percent of the human race. All we say to the individual is, "Be three feet back of your head." If he is, he orients himself, he knows that he is not his body, he knows he does not have to be up against his reactive mind, he has been gotten out of the trap. Of course, there are many other things which you could do to further increase his ability and orient him in this position, but this is not immediately in our province in Dianetics. When an individual is so exteriorized he also can look over the body and patch up pinched nerves, black areas, rearrange the anchor points which create and hold the space of the body, and so repair a body quite excellently. However, it is not the purpose of exteriorization simply to get a person to square away[1] the machine known as a body.

"Be three feet back of your head" is a strange and interesting combination of words. Evidently this simple combination has not been known before by man. It is notable that one does not say, "Move three feet back of your head," since an awareness of awareness unit does not move, it appears and disappears from locations.

If one uses this "One-Shot Clear" technique, he should be advised that he must not ask or expect of the newly exteriorized person a number of strange or impossible things. He must not ask him to go chasing around finding things. He must not ask him to prove that he is exteriorized. The individual says so — that's the end of it. In Scientology, of course, on Route 1, as contained in *The Creation of Human Ability,* we go on to improve the ability of this exteriorized awareness of awareness unit up to a point which we call "Operating Thetan."[2] We do this by running many drills and exercises which improve his perception. However, the process of Answers, or even the six basic processes can be run on the individual after he is exteriorized and his exteriorization will markedly increase, and he will get into even better condition as an exteriorized person. If you were to say "Be

---

1. **square away:** to get ready; to put in order.

2. **Operating Thetan:** it is a state of beingness. It is a being "at cause over matter, energy, space, time, form and life." *Operating* comes from "able to operate without dependency on things," and *thetan* is the Greek letter theta (θ), which the Greeks used to represent *thought* or perhaps *spirit,* to which an *n* is added to make a noun in the modern style used to create words in engineering. It is also θ^n or "theta to the nth degree," meaning unlimited or vast.

three feet back of your head" to somebody, and he was, the next thing to do would be to go into Elementary Straightwire, then into Opening Procedure of 8-C, then Opening Procedure by Duplication, then Remedy of Havingness, then Spotting Spots in Space, and then Answers, or, as the last chapter gives forth, "Remedy of Communication." If you did these things just as given in this book you would have something like a stable Clear. You would pay no attention to the fact that he was Clear. As a matter of fact, if you were to run any of these six basic processes long enough, and certainly if you were to run Answers for any length of time after you have run these six basic processes, you would have somebody exteriorized. It is a peculiar thing that there is no argument about exteriorization. Any argument which has been in existence was born out of the psychiatrist's observation of "compulsive exteriorization" by an individual so detesting his body that he stayed outside of it. Psychiatrists have been known to give people electric shocks and other "treatments" to get them to get back inside their body. This level of punishment— trying to get a person to accept something under duress—does not work. But then, nothing in psychiatry ever worked, except bank accounts. This "compulsive exteriorization" is a manifestation which we call in Scientology "doing a bunk," in other words, running away. You will occasionally encounter this, but you will not encounter it if you run the six basic processes before you go in for exteriorization.

There is, astonishingly enough, a "One-command Clear" for the remaining fifty percent, even if it has to be repeated many times. I have been developing and testing this for some time, and have kept it back on the shelf against a time when we had enough competent auditors to use a process intelligently.

This is a "One-Shot Clear" technique in that one uses one command and so achieves clearing, and after clearing till the stage of exteriorization has been accomplished, one simply goes on using the same type of command. It is a highly effective process, a very violent process. Theoretically it would work on any level of case. In actual practice psychotic, neurotic cases, or people badly out of communication receive it with considerable difficulty and it is not recommended for them, but it would work on them if it could be communicated to them. (On such people use Opening Procedure of 8-C, only.)

The basis for this process is the observation that the MEST universe is a game. One can have a game and know it. He can be in a game and not know it. The difference is his determinism.

Games require space and havingness. A game requires other players. Games also require skill and knowingness that they are games.

Havingness is the need to have terminals and things to play for and on.

When a game is done the player keeps around tokens. These are hopes the game will start again. When that hope is dead the token, the terminal, is hidden. And it becomes an automaticity—a game going on below the level of knowingness. Truthfully, one never stops playing a game once started. He plays old games in secret—even from himself—while playing or not playing new ones. The only *real* game one can have is in present time. All others are in the past or in the future. Anxiety for a game takes one into the past.

The command is, "Invent a game," and when the preclear has, again, "Invent a game." Then: "Mock up somebody else inventing a game."

Having established the fact that an auditing session is in progress, and established some slight communication with the preclear, the auditor says, "Invent a game." When the communication lag on this is flat, the auditor then uses the command, "Mock up somebody else inventing a game." This is the only phrase he utters, but he of course engages in two-way communication with the preclear when the preclear has something to say to him. An auditor has to be a good auditor in order to use this process. Just because it is a simple "one-command" process is no reason why it will work for an auditor who is not cognizant of the Auditor's Code, cognizant of a two-way communication and has some experience in more basic levels of processing.

We use this process as a remedy for the scarcity of games and we use it in full awareness of the processes involved in two-way communication.

It is a murderous process and requires five to ten hours in rough cases to bring about an understanding of existence.

This is not necessarily a recommended process. It is a workable process, it does function, it is fast, but remember that it has the frailty of the ability of the auditor himself. It has the frailty of failing when a two-way communication is not maintained with the preclear. It will fail if the preclear, in volunteering information, finds no attention from the auditor. It will fail if the auditor does not acknowledge the fact that the preclear has done this. But, if these things are considered, it will work.

This process can be abused by the preclear. He can wander from it. He can sit there in the auditing chair doing other things, but we depend upon the skill of the auditor to see that the preclear is not doing other things, and that he is actually doing the process.

The preclear will "pick his bank clean" rather than invent, he will have doubts that he *is* inventing. But we persevere and we win.

15

ARC Processing

15

ARC Processing

If we examine communication we will discover that all communication lag is the introduction of matter, energy, space and time into communication. The more time has been introduced into communication, the less communication there is.

As an example of this, let us say that a star in some other galaxy explodes, and then let us trace the length of time necessary for a small amount of that explosion's particles to reach Earth across great space. Almost countless light-years elapse before this communication line has been completed. This is a very, very long communication. Not necessarily a communication lag since the progress of the particles is not interrupted. There are no vias. Actually, MEST itself does not have a communication lag, it is totally a communication lag.

The more this sort of thing enters into communication, the worse off is the preclear. Thus we can see that the subject of MEST itself is the aberrative factor.

As we examine barriers, we find that they are matter, energy, space and time. We discover that we can overcome the barriers of matter, we can climb the walls or go through them. We can somehow or other brave or get on the other side of energy barriers. We discover that even space has limitations even when it appears as limitless as the space of this universe (and the space of this universe appears as big as a person supposes it is big, whereas actually it is, to a thetan who can get outside of it, about the size of a matchbox to a child). The one barrier which we could discover difficult to get around is time.

The basic definitions and understanding of matter, energy, space and time are not particularly germane in this place. They are taken up on a much higher theoretical level in Scientology, but the essence of time is that it is measured or marked by the motion of particles in space. Space and energy particles are necessary to have mechanical time, but what is time, basically? Time is actually a consideration. There is time because one considers there is time.

You must examine the physical universe very closely to discover that the reason it is always here is because it is, each and every particle of it, each cubic inch of space of it, in *forever*. The physical universe is not moving through time, it is stuck in time. Each and every part of it is fixed in a *now* which lasts forever. The only real changes which take place in the physical universe are those introduced into it by life. We can argue about this if we want to but we are interested here in a concept which leads toward a workable process.

We discover that time exists for the individual to the degree that the individual makes time. Time is the other-determined thing to nearly everyone alive. He depends on clocks, he depends on the rising and setting of the sun, he depends on all manner of mechanisms to tell him what is time. Actually the more a person is told what time is, the more he gets into a dependency upon some other consideration, and so he drops into forever. When he stops considering that he is making time, when he stops making time by considerations, he is dropping himself into a foreverness. He has less and less motion, he has less and less determinism. Time is a very insidious barrier because its apparency would tell an individual that time is created by the movement of things. Actually it is not, it is created by a consideration that things are moving.

The remedy of the barrier of time produces an astonishing effect upon a preclear. When the auditor is auditing one of these "One-Shot Clear" commands (the one given in the last chapter and the one given in this chapter) he will stumble across quite a bit of complication on the subject of time. An individual told to have some complications by decision will eventually move out into the fact that the most complicated thing he can get into is time, and so this is a very satisfactory game. We can process this factor directly.

This process is the essence of simplicity. It has one command. The command is "Make some time." This is all the command there is. One does not advise or teach the preclear how to make some time. One accepts whatever the preclear decides makes time as the answer. One maintains the two-way communication with the preclear, and answers comments which the preclear has on it. One carefully does not evaluate for the preclear and tell him how to make some time. One does not set an example in making time. One simply has the preclear make some time.

This process on some cases has to be run many hours before the preclear comes into partial control of the barrier of time. When he does this he of course comes into some control of his engram bank and his considerations.

The making of time naturally puts into motion all those silent or motionless masses which are hanging to the preclear and which actually pin together his reactive bank.

This is an enormous joke upon the preclear himself and the universe that he makes all the time he will ever perceive. He cannot possibly get out of phase with "forever" if he is in contact with the foreverness of space and energy masses of which this universe is composed. When he starts to protest against the universe at large he starts to protest against the foreverness which includes all time, and so he withdraws into earlier times when he was making time in order to have some himself.

"Make some time," is a process of astonishing ramifications.

But remember, time is a barrier. One could also say, "Make some space," "Make some energy," "Make some objects," "Make some terminals," and have gains in a preclear. But these are barriers. Although a game requires barriers, the preclear already has too many in the past, too few in the present.

Barriers are not life.

We must use three cardinal rules in processing:

1. Process toward truth.

2. Process toward ability.

3. Process toward life.

Auditing commands must emphasize truth, ability, life.

Don't process toward entheta, chronic somatics, difficulties. Ignore them.

The only thing wrong with the preclear is that his attention is fixed on barriers—*MEST*. His freedom depends upon putting his attention on freedom or present time. Here are two auditing commands. Which is correct?

1. "Find some things you can't do."

2. "Find some things you can do."

The second is correct. The first will almost spin a preclear. Why? Because it concentrates on a lie. A preclear can do anything!

A preclear has a bad leg. Which is the right process?

1. "Touch the back of your chair."

2. "Recall a time when somebody hurt his leg."

The first is correct. It is *faster*. Why? Because it processes toward ability.

We have a preclear who is apathetic. Which process is the right one?

1. "Who used to have headaches?" or

2. "Feel the floor beneath your feet."

The second is correct because it processes toward life, not illness.

That which the auditor concentrates upon in auditing comes true. Hence, the processing of MEST gives us new barriers. The processing of life gives new life.

Processing barriers gives us *limited* processes. Processing life gives us *unlimited* processes. Life is composed of affinity, reality, communication. These make understanding. Modern ARC Processing processes communication as given earlier in this volume. ARC Processing includes the following powerful processes:

1. "Tell me something you might communicate with." "Tell me something that would communicate with you."

2. "What might you agree with?" "What might agree with you?"

3. "Tell me something you would like." "Tell me something that might like you."

These are present time, not past or future processes. They produce very strong reactions. They solve *very* rough cases. They are summed in a simple process which does not dispense with them: "Tell me something (someone) you could understand." "Tell me something (someone) who could understand you."

Note - Of course a very basic process which resolves chronic somatics, eye difficulties, any specific item is to have the affected part or bad area of energy say "hello" and "okay" and "all right" until it is in good condition — not that an auditor should address specific conditions — LRH

16

Exteriorization

16

Exteriorization

The auditor will be confronted with a great many problems of exteriorization once he has exteriorized his preclear. The things not to do and to do are as follows:

1. Do not require the awareness of awareness unit to again put its attention on the body.

2. Do not make a person prove that he is exteriorized.

3. Do not make a newly exteriorized person discover, find things, read the future or do other nonsensical tricks.

4. Maintain the Auditor's Code more severely than before.

5. Continue the process in which the preclear exteriorized.

If the auditor knows these things he will not get the preclear and himself into trouble. The auditing command "Be three feet back of your head," sometimes gets the auditor into more trouble than he is equipped to handle. A preclear may do a compulsive exteriorization, "do a bunk," or drop his body limp in the chair and give from that body no sign that he is hearing any of the auditing commands given by the auditor. One such case was pleaded with for half an hour by an auditor along the lines that the preclear should remember her husband, should think of her children, should come back and live for the sake of her friends, and found no response from the preclear. Finally the auditor said, "Think of your poor auditor," at which moment the preclear promptly returned.

A limited "compulsive exteriorization" is the preclear going out of the body and getting plastered against the ceiling, or falling in terror upward into the sky (an inverting of gravity). This manifestation is equally upsetting.

If a preclear has been given the command "Be three feet back of your head," and if he "does a bunk," or if he "falls out of the body upward," all the auditor has to do is get into two-way communication with the preclear. Actually, he should have, as an auditor, an excellent command of the Chart of Human Evaluation of *Science of Survival*. He would then not tell a preclear below 2.0 on the Tone Scale to "Be three feet back of your head," for when they do, at these lower levels of the Tone Scale, it is on a compulsive or obsessive level, and all the preclear can think of is to try and get away.

Another remedy, if this untoward[1] and strange occurrence happens, is to ask the preclear to

"Reach from your position to your body,"

"Withdraw from the body,"

"Reach for the body,"

"Withdraw from the body" or

"Decide to run away and run away," several times.

---

1. **untoward:** unfavorable and unfortunate.

Remember, such things as this occur only when the auditor has not placed his preclear on the Tone Scale before he began to audit him.

The way to get away from these entirely is to audit the six basic processes on the preclear, and then audit either or both of the "One-Shot Clear" processes of remedying Communication and Time Processing until the preclear exteriorizes and then simply go right on auditing the process which exteriorized the preclear. Remember that a preclear exteriorized is simply an awareness of awareness unit which has been taken out of a trap, and the awareness of awareness unit has not changed any from the basic individual, but now recognizes itself to be out of the trap and is quite happy about it.

A very funny manifestation occurs on some very low-toned preclears when they talk about exteriorization. They say, "I'm over *there*." This, of course, is impossible. An individual is always *here*. It is here where you are. Lord knows what this individual who says "I'm over there" has exteriorized—a circuit, a mock-up, some such thing. He himself definitely is not. Another manifestation we have is "buttered all over the universe." A preclear who is buttered all over the universe is one who does not know where he is and if we ask him many, many times, over and over and over, each time making him get a spot with certainty, "Can you find a spot where you are not?" we will gradually narrow down his area. What has actually happened in such a case is that the preclear has used remote viewpoints,[2] and has left remote viewpoints located all over everywhere to such a degree that the preclear thinks he is any place rather than where he is.

---

2. **remote viewpoints:** those viewpoints which an individual puts out remotely, to look through.

The main thing one has to know about exteriorization is that it takes place. If one uses the six basic processes, remembers the Auditor's Code, and the two "One-Shot Clear" processes, he is then quite safe on exteriorization, for it will occur when it occurs, and the thing to do after it occurs is to do the same process one has been doing when it occurs or to run the six basic processes while exteriorized, or follow *The Creation of Human Ability* Route 1. Of course, one should acknowledge the fact of the preclear's mentioning it and one should certainly permit the preclear to discuss it, but one should continue with the process which exteriorized him, unless, of course, one is very well trained in exteriorization exercises.

As exteriorization drilling, as an activity, is most germane to the realm of Scientology, further knowledge of it and about it is written up in *The Creation of Human Ability*. Here are given the Route 1 steps which should be run after an exteriorization takes place.

The creation of a Clear undertaken in 1950 actually was this manifestation of exteriorization happening at some random moment and not being adequately cared for after it occurred. Nobody remarked upon the fact that he was a distance from the body because most of the people who were thus exteriorized had very good visio on their own banks but very poor visio on the immediate environment. A little more exteriorization work and any one of these Clears would have suddenly found themselves out into the room looking at the room directly without the aid of eyes.

We wanted Clears in 1950. We still want Clears. This is the way to make them, the way to make them stable, the way to make anybody you process far more able.

The byword on this is not to address specific errors or

difficulties, but to validate abilities and process immediately toward the acquisition of further and further and higher abilities. We are not in there to pay attention to all the bad things in the world, since these are composed only of the imaginings of the individual. Let us increase the ability of the individual to create, to be, to perceive, and increase his ability to associate all along the dynamics. If we should do this it would be a far, far better world.

finis

About the Author

About the Author

L. Ron Hubbard is one of the most acclaimed and widely read authors of all time, primarily because his works express a firsthand knowledge of the nature of man—knowledge gained not from standing on the sidelines but through lifelong experience with people from all walks of life.

As Ron said, "One doesn't learn about life by sitting in an ivory tower, thinking about it. One learns about life by being part of it." And that is how he lived.

He began his quest for knowledge on the nature of man at a very early age. When he was eight years old he was already well on his way to being a seasoned traveler, covering a quarter of a million miles by the age of nineteen. His adventures included voyages to China, Japan and other points in the Orient and South Pacific. During this time he became closely acquainted with twenty-one different races in areas all over the world.

After returning to the United States, Ron pursued his formal studies of mathematics and engineering at George Washington University, where he was also a member of one of the first classes on nuclear physics. He realized that neither the East nor the West contained the full answer to the problems of existence.

Despite all of mankind's advances in the physical sciences, a *workable* technology of the mind and life had never been developed. The mental "technologies" which did exist, psychology and psychiatry, were actually barbaric, false subjects—no more workable than the methods of jungle witch doctors. Ron shouldered the responsibility of filling this gap in the knowledge of mankind.

He financed his early research through fiction writing. He became one of the most highly demanded authors in the golden age of popular adventure and science fiction writing during the 1930s and 1940s, interrupted only by his service in the U.S. Navy during World War II.

Partially disabled at the war's end, Ron applied what he had learned from his researches. He made breakthroughs and developed techniques which made it possible for him to recover from his injuries and help others to regain their health. It was during this time that the basic tenets of Dianetics technology were codified.

A year later, in 1948, he wrote the first manuscript detailing his discoveries. Ron did not have it published at that time, but gave copies to some friends who copied it and passed it among their friends, who then passed it on to others. (This book was published in 1951 as *Dianetics: The Original Thesis* and later republished as *The Dynamics of Life*.) The interest generated by this manuscript prompted a flood of requests for more information on the subject.

Ron attempted to make all his discoveries available to the American Psychiatric Association and the American Medical Association. Despite the fact that his work would have benefited these groups immensely, his offers were met with disinterest. He therefore decided to write a comprehensive text on the subject and take it directly to the public.

With the publication of *Dianetics: The Modern Science of Mental Health* on May 9, 1950, a complete handbook for the application of Ron's new technology was broadly available for the first time. *Dianetics* created a wildfire of public interest. The book immediately shot to the top of the New York Times bestseller list and stayed there week after week. More than 750 Dianetics study groups sprang up within a few short months of its publication.

Ron kept on researching, improving methods and developing ways to advance other people's ability to apply Dianetics technology.

At the end of 1954, L. Ron Hubbard released one of his most significant breakthroughs: the communication formula. For the first time the anatomy and mechanics of communication were clearly and concisely stated. In all history many men had written about communication, debated about it, moralized about it and theorized about it. But before L. Ron Hubbard, no one had ever isolated the essential component parts of communication.

Ron found that skilled handling of communication played a vital part in any successful application of processing techniques, as well as to a person's success in getting along in life.

"A man is as dead as he can't communicate," Ron wrote. "He is as alive as he can communicate. With countless tests, I have discovered to a degree which could be called conclusive, that the only remedy for living is further communication. One must add to his ability to communicate."

Ron's work did not stop with the successes of Dianetics. Further research led him to the basic truths of life itself and from these discoveries he developed Scientology, the first totally workable technology for the improvement of life.

The number of books and lectures continued to grow for more than three decades as Ron kept on with his research into the mind and life.

Today Ron's works—including an astounding number of books, taped lectures, instructional films, writings, demonstrations and briefings—are studied and applied daily. Dianetics and Scientology techniques are used in hundreds of Hubbard Dianetics Foundations and Scientology organizations on every continent.

With his research fully completed and codified, L. Ron Hubbard departed his body on January 24, 1986.

Ron's work opened a new door for mankind. Through his efforts, there now exists a totally workable technology with which people can help each other improve their lives and succeed in achieving their goals.

Millions of people all over the world consider they have no truer friend.

Glossary

Abstractacity: quality of being difficult to understand.

abstracts: ideas or terms considered apart from some material basis or objects.

Acceptance Level Processes: the five stages of Acceptance Level Processing. One has the preclear mock up, no matter how blackly or how crudely, items for himself to accept; then have others in his mock-ups mock up things for them to accept, and others to mock up things for others to accept. This extends to having the preclear also mock up things for others to accept and others to mock up things for the preclear to accept.

Adler: Alfred Adler (1870–1937) Viennese psychologist who opposed Freud's emphasis on sex and advanced his own theory of the inferiority complex to explain psychopathic cases.

Alexander: Alexander III (356–23 b.c.), also known as Alexander the Great, king of Macedonia, an ancient kingdom located in what is now Greece and Yugoslavia.

anchor points: points which demark the outermost boundaries of a space or its corners.

as-ised: viewed exactly as it is, without any distortions or lies, at which moment it vanishes and ceases to exist.

atomic pile: an early name for a nuclear reactor (an apparatus in which a nuclear fission chain reaction can be initiated, sustained and controlled, for generating heat or producing useful radiation). *See also* **fission** in this Glossary.

auditor: a person trained and qualified in applying Dianetics and/or Scientology processes and procedures to individuals for their betterment; called an *auditor* because auditor means "one who listens."

awareness of awareness unit: an actuality of no mass, no wavelength, no position in space or relation in time, but with the quality of creating or destroying mass or energy, of locating itself or creating space and in re-relating time.

Babylon: ancient city which was the capital of Babylonia, an ancient empire in southwest Asia in what is now southern Iraq. It flourished between 2100 and 689 B.C.

basal metabolism: the basic chemical change in the body between oxygen and fuel. It tells you if the preclear really is eating, or has eaten breakfast. (For further information on basal metabolism, read the book *E-Meter Essentials*.)

Bennington: a battle of the American Revolutionary War in which U.S. troops defeated the British. It was fought in 1777 near Bennington, Vermont.

blind alley: a situation offering no chance for progress or improvement.

book auditor: someone who has successfully applied Scientology from a book to help someone else and who has been certified for doing so.

botany: the science that deals with plants, their life, structure, growth, classification, etc.

capital: owners of wealth used in business collectively: distinguished from labor.

central organization: a Scientology service organization.

Chaldean: of Chaldea, an ancient province of Babylonia, approximately 1100–539 B.C. *See also* **Babylon** in this Glossary.

charlatan: a person who pretends to have expert knowledge or skill that he doesn't have; a fake.

Chart of Human Evaluation: a chart organized in very early 1951 by L. Ron Hubbard. It has various columns and gives behavior characteristics. It is plotted out mathematically on the basis of ARC; a very good chart to use in order to predict people. (For further information on this chart, read Ron's book *Science of Survival.*)

circuit: a division of your own mind that seems to make up another personality and this other personality affects you, argues with you and so forth.

cleared: brought to the state of Clear. The name of a state achieved through auditing or an individual who has achieved this state. A Clear is a being who no longer has his own reactive mind. A Clear is an unaberrated person and is rational in that he forms the best possible solutions he can on the data he has and from his viewpoint. The Clear has no engrams which can be restimulated to throw out the correctness of computation by entering hidden and false data.

common coin: something that is current through being commonly mentioned, discussed or accepted.

common denominator: a quality, attribute, opinion, etc., shared by all the persons or things in a group.

communication lag: the length of time intervening between the posing of the question, or origination of a statement, and the exact moment that question or original statement is answered.

conundrum: any puzzling question or problem.

cubist: refers to *cubism*, a technique of writing that attempts to exploit abstract structural relationships of things by using bizarre associations and dissociations in imagery, the simultaneous evocation of several points of view toward the material, and other devices.

delineated: outlined or described.

detonative: tending to explode violently and noisily.

disenfranchised: deprived of a privilege, right or power.

dust-binned: ash-canned; garbage-canned.

dwindling spiral: a phenomenon of the ARC triangle whereby when one breaks some affinity, a little bit of the reality goes down, and then communication goes down, which makes it impossible to get affinity as high as before; so a little bit more gets knocked off affinity, and then reality goes down, and then communication. This is the dwindling spiral in progress, until it hits the bottom—death—which is no affinity, no communication and no reality.

dyed-in-the-wool: thoroughgoing; unchanging.

egress: the act of going out or forth; emergence.

Elementary Straightwire: a basic process with two commands: "Give me something you wouldn't mind remembering," "Give me something you wouldn't mind forgetting."

E-Meter: an electronic device for measuring the mental state or change of state of *Homo sapiens*. It is *not* a lie detector. It does not diagnose or cure anything. It is used by auditors to assist the preclear in locating areas of spiritual distress or travail.

emotional scale: *See* **Tone Scale** in this Glossary.

engram: a mental image picture which is a recording of an experience containing pain, unconsciousness and a real or fancied threat to survival. It is a recording in the reactive mind of something which actually happened to an individual in the past and which contained pain and unconsciousness, both of which are recorded in the mental image picture called an engram. It must, by definition, have impact or injury as part of its content. These engrams are a complete recording, down to the last accurate detail, of every perception present in a moment of partial or full unconsciousness.

equanimity: the quality of remaining calm and undisturbed; evenness of mind or temper; composure.

erasure: the action of erasing (rubbing out) locks, secondaries or engrams.

esoteric: intended only for people with special knowledge or interest.

essayed: tried; attempted.

euthanasia: the original definition of *euthanasia* is "mercy killing" or "easy death." However, under the practice of psychiatry it has become "the act of killing people considered a burden on society."

evaluate: to impose data or knowledge upon another. An example would be someone telling another why he is the way he is instead of permitting or guiding him to discover it for himself.

fission: atomic fission: the splitting of the nucleus of an atom accompanied by conversion of part of the mass into energy. This is the principle of the atomic bomb.

Freudian Analysis: Freud's methods in psychoanalysis. Psychoanalysis: a system of mental therapy developed by Sigmund Freud [(1856-1939) Austrian physician and neurologist; founder of psychoanalysis] in Austria in 1894 and which depends upon the following practices for its effects: the patient is made to talk about and recall his childhood for years while the practitioner brings about a transfer of the patient's personality to his own and searches for hidden sexual incidents believed by Freud to be the only cause of aberration; the practitioner reads sexual significances into all statements and evaluates them for the patient along sexual lines. Each of these points later proved to be based on false premises and incomplete research, accounting for their lack of results and the subsequent failure of the subject and its offshoots.

gamut: the entire range or extent of something.

germinated: started developing or growing.

glut: a supply of certain goods that is greater than the demand.

havingness: the concept of being able to reach. By *havingness* is meant owning, possessing, being capable of commanding, taking charge of objects, energies and spaces.

Hubbard Association of Scientologists International (HASI): the general membership group of the church at the time of this book. It was open to individuals who used Scientology procedures to improve themselves and others. It has since been replaced as a membership group by the International Association of Scientologists (IAS). At the time this book was written, the HASI also handled the publication of materials, provided professional training and processing services and additionally functioned as a research and investigation unit.

Hubbard Certified Auditor (HCA): a person who has completed a course of auditor training specializing in Scientology theory and application as part of the Phoenix Certification Course in late 1954. Today, an HCA is known as a Class II auditor.

Hubbard Dianetic Auditor (HDA): a person who has completed auditor training specializing in Dianetics theory and application in the Phoenix Certification Course in late 1954. Today, an HDA is a person who completes the Hubbard Dianetics Auditor Course.

ingress: the act of entering.

innuendoes: indirect remarks, gestures or references usually implying something derogatory.

insidious: operating in a slow or not easily apparent manner; more dangerous than seems evident.

interiorized: having gone into something too fixedly and become part of it too fixedly.

jaw-cracking: hard to pronounce.

Kant, Immanuel: (1724–1804) German philosopher, said that man had a section of knowledge called unknowable.

Keats: John Keats (1795–1821), English poet, considered one of the greatest English poets. His poems are unequaled for dignity, melody and richness of imagery.

Komroff, Manuel: (1890–1974) American writer born in New York City.

libido theory: a theory originated in 1894 by Sigmund Freud which states that all life impulses and behaviors are sex-motivated.

lock: a mental image picture of a nonpainful but disturbing experience the person has had, which depends for its force on earlier secondaries and engrams which the experience has restimulated (stirred up).

Marathon: a plain in southeast Greece where the Athenians defeated the Persians in 490 B.C.

mathematicity: the state or condition of being mathematical.

mock up: knowingly create a mental image picture that is not part of the time track.

modus operandi: mode of operation; way of doing or making; procedure.

moot: so hypothetical as to be meaningless.

mysticism: a doctrine of an immediate spiritual intuition of truths believed to transcend ordinary understanding, or of a direct, intimate union of the soul with God through contemplation or ecstasy.

non sequitur: not following; an unrelated or illogical statement or conclusion.

north: in the direction of case improvement.

nuclear physicists: scientists in that branch of physics which deals with atoms, their nuclear structure and the behavior of nuclear particles.

nymphomania: abnormal and uncontrollable desire by a woman for sexual intercourse.

One-Shot Clear: the one phrase or one action given once, or repeated, which would bring into being the Clear as described in *Dianetics: The Modern Science of Mental Health*.

onslaught: a violent, intense attack.

Opening Procedure by Duplication: a Scientology process. It has as its goal the separating of time, moment from moment. This is done by getting a preclear to duplicate his same action over and over again with two dissimilar objects. In England this process is called "Book and Bottle," probably because these two familiar objects are the most used in doing Opening Procedure by Duplication.

Opening Procedure of 8-C: consists of having the preclear move his body around the room under the auditor's direction until (a) he finds he is in actual communication with many spots on the surface of things in the room, (b) until he can select spots in the room and know he is selecting them and can communicate with them, and (c) select spots and move to them, decide when to touch them and when to let go. *8-C* is the number of another process and is also used to mean good control.

Operating Thetan: it is a state of beingness. It is a being "at cause over matter, energy, space, time, form and life." *Operating* comes from "able to operate without dependency on things," and *Thetan* is the Greek letter Theta (θ), which the Greeks used to represent *thought* or perhaps *spirit*, to which an *n* is added to make a noun in the modern style used to create words in engineering. It is also θ^n or "theta to the nth degree," meaning unlimited or vast.

ostensibly: apparently; seemingly.

PABs: Professional Auditor's Bulletins. These are issues written by L. Ron Hubbard between 10 May 1953 and 15 May 1959.

The content of these bulletins are technical and promotional. Their intent is to give the professional auditor and his preclears the best possible processes and processing available at the moment it becomes available.

Perfect Duplication: a process by which a preclear is gotten to create a perfect duplicate of an object. A perfect duplicate is an additional creation of the object, its energy and space, in its own space, in its own time, using its own energy.

perforce: by or through necessity; necessarily.

perusal: the act of reading.

Pilate, Pontius: first century A.D. Roman prosecutor who condemned Jesus to be crucified. According to the Bible he attempted to not be responsible for Jesus' death by publicly washing his hands and giving responsibility to a mob of people who were calling for Jesus' death.

pilloried: exposed to ridicule, public contempt, scorn or abuse.

platform: a statement of principles and policies.

poliomyelitis: inflammation of the gray matter of the spinal cord. Certain forms of the disease produce muscular paralysis and atrophy, others do not.

preclear: a spiritual being who is now on the road to becoming Clear, hence pre-Clear.

predicated: founded (a statement, action, etc.) or based upon.

prima donna: the principal woman singer in an opera or concert.

process: a set of questions asked or commands given by an auditor to help a person find out things about himself or life and to improve his condition.

processing: the application of Dianetics or Scientology processes to someone by a trained auditor. The exact definition of processing is: the action of asking a preclear a question (which he can understand and answer), getting an answer to that question and acknowledging him for that answer. Also called *auditing*.

provisos: conditions or stipulations.

psychosomatic: *psycho* refers to mind and *somatic* refers to body; the term *psychosomatic* means the mind making the body ill or illnesses which have been created physically within the body by derangement of the mind.

Q and A: the practice of asking a question about a pc's answer, i.e., the auditor asks a question, the pc answers, the auditor asks a question about the answer. This is the chief auditor fault, as it is giving session control over to the pc. The auditor following only the pc's lead is giving no auditing and the pc is left on "self-audit." Here is a wrong example of auditing: *Auditor:* "How are you?" *Pc:* "Awful." *Auditor:* "What's wrong?" Here is a right example: *Auditor:* "How are you?" *Pc:* "Awful." *Auditor:* "Thank you."

reactive mind: that portion of a person's mind which works on a totally stimulus-response basis, which is not under his volitional control and which exerts force and the power of command over his awareness, purposes, thoughts, body and actions. The reactive mind is where engrams are stored.

regimen: a certain, settled schedule of things.

Remedy of Havingness: a process that has a preclear mock up a mass in front of him and shove it into his body, and mock up another mass in front of him and throw it away, over and over. When the process has been done thoroughly and completely, the preclear should be able to reject or accept, at his own discretion, anything in his environment as well as anything in his engram bank.

remote viewpoints: those viewpoints which an individual puts out remotely, to look through.

restimulation: reactivation of a past memory due to similar circumstances in the present approximating circumstances of the past.

restimulators: anything in the individual's surroundings which is sufficiently similar to something in his reactive mind that it causes part of his reactive mind to become restimulated.

reverable: worthy of being regarded with deep respect, love and awe.

rigorous: rigidly precise; thoroughly accurate or exact.

rocket jockey: an astronaut.

rostrum: any platform, stage, etc., for public speaking.

sacrosanct: above or beyond change, criticism or interference.

Saki: pen name for Hector Hugo Munro (1870–1916) English short story writer and novelist, known for his witty, often bizarre stories.

satyrism: state or condition of uncontrollable sexual desire in men.

saving grace: quality that makes up for other generally negative characteristics.

Scientology: Scientology applied religious philosophy. It is the study and handling of the spirit in relationship to itself, universes and other life. Scientology means *scio*, knowing in the fullest sense of the word, and *logos*, study. In itself the word means literally "knowing how to know." Scientology is a "route," a way, rather than a dissertation or an assertive body of knowledge. Through its drills and studies one may find the truth for himself. The technology is therefore not expounded as something to believe, but something to *do*.

secondary: also called *secondary engram*. A period of anguish brought about by a major loss or threat of loss to the individual. The secondary engram depends for its strength and force upon physical-pain engrams which underlie it.

servomechanism: a mechanism which serves, services or aids something.

session: a precise period of time during which an auditor audits a preclear.

shaman's: belonging to a priest or medicine man of shamanism (shamanism is the religion of certain peoples of northeast Asia, based on a belief in good and evil spirits who can be influenced only by the shamans).

signalizes: makes clearly known; draws attention to.

south: out the bottom, losing, etc.

spiritualism: the belief that the dead survive as spirits which can communicate with the living, especially with the help of a third party.

Spotting Spots in Space: a process in which the goal is to bring the preclear to a point where he can spot locations in space which do not have color, mass or shape but which are simply locations, and spot that same location repeatedly without variation.

square away: to get ready; to put in order.

stimulus-response: given a certain stimulus something will automatically give a certain response.

stir-crazy: mentally ill because of long imprisonment.

Straightwire: the name of a process. It is the act of stringing a line between present time and some incident in the past, and stringing that line directly and without any detours. The auditor is stringing a straight "wire" of memory between the actual genus (origin) of a condition and present time, thus demonstrating that there is a difference of time and space in the condition then and the condition now, and that the preclear, conceding this difference, then rids himself of the condition or at least is able to handle it.

surplice: a loose, white, wide-sleeved outer garment worn by the clergy and choir of some churches.

symbolic logic: a system for applying the principles of mathematics to logical reasoning, using symbols to represent exact relationships between concepts.

Tanganyika, Lake: lake in east central Africa 420 miles long, between 30 and 45 miles wide with a maximum depth of 4710 feet.

telekinesis: the ability to move or deform inanimate objects through mental processes.

theta: energy peculiar to life or a thetan which acts upon material in the physical universe and animates it, mobilizes it and changes it; natural creative energy of a thetan which he has free to direct toward survival goals, especially when it manifests itself as high tone, constructive communications.

Tone Scale: a scale which shows the emotional tones of a person. These, ranged from the highest to the lowest, are, in part, serenity, enthusiasm (as we proceed downward), conservatism, boredom, antagonism, anger, covert hostility, fear, grief, apathy.

tractor-type beams: energy flows that pull things towards their source.

Univacs: *Trademark* electronic computing devices. [from Univ(ersal) A(utomatic) C(omputer)].

unswervably: in a manner not turning aside in movement or direction; not deviating from the straight or direct course.

untoward: unfavorable and unfortunate.

vested interest: the person or group, etc., who benefits the most from existing business or financial systems.

viewpoint: a point from which to view.

visio: the recall of something seen, so that it is seen again in the mind in full color, scale, dimension, brightness and detail.

vitals: the essential parts of something.

Waterloo: a battle on 18 June 1815, near the town of Waterloo, in central Belgium, in which the British and the Prussians decisively defeated Napoleon and ended his power.

wended: traveled.

Index

Aberration(s), aberrate(d),
common denominator of all
neurosis, psychosis,
aberration and
psychosomatic ills is "can't
work," 65
communication flow, 96
communication line, 106
defined, 99
defined in terms of
communication, 105
Dianetics, control over
aberration, 63
violations in communication
formula, 116

ability,
accent on ability, 53
as communication, 95
control, part of understanding
and ability, 61
fear of loss of ability, 59
raising ability, 34
subdivisions in life, ability and
mechanics, 21

acknowledgment,
execution of commands, 135
importance in processing, 126–7
lack of, effect on case, 135

acknowledgment lag, 134

Adler, 111

affinity, precision definition, 55;
see also **ARC**

analytical mind, 25
defined and described, 26

anger, communication and, 55

answer hunger, unfinished
communication, 99

ARC,
component parts of freedom, 91
life, understanding and ARC, 56
no freedom in absence of ARC,
90

ARC Processing, 203

ARC triangle, 54

astral walking, confusing
exteriorization with, 41

audit(ing), processing,
activity of creating a Clear, 43
commands must emphasize
truth, ability, life, 206
communication, 181
no auditing without two-way
communication, 161
originating communications,
135
three cardinal rules, 206

auditor(s),
gives power to everything he
validates, 162
greatest frailty of auditors, 73

Books and Tapes
by L. Ron Hubbard

Dianetics Graduate Books

You've read *Dianetics 55!* Now get the rest of the Dianetics Graduate Books Package. These books by L. Ron Hubbard give you detailed knowledge of how the mind works—data you can use to help yourself and others break out of the traps of life. While you can get these books individually, the Dianetics Graduate Books Package can be also purchased as a set, complete with an attractive slipcase.

Science of Survival • If you ever wondered how people act the way they do, you'll find this book a wealth of information. It's vital to anyone who wants to understand others and improve personal relationships. *Science of Survival* is built around a remarkable chart—The Hubbard Chart of Human Evaluation. With it you can understand and predict other people's behavior and reactions and greatly increase your control over your own life. This is a valuable handbook that can make a difference between success and failure on the job and in life.

Advanced Procedure and Axioms • For the *first* time the basics of thought and the physical universe have been codified into a set of fundamental laws, signaling an entirely new way to view and approach the subjects of man, the physical universe and even life itself.

Handbook for Preclears • Written as an advanced personal workbook, *Handbook for Preclears* contains easily done processes to help you overcome the effect of times you were not in control of your life, times that your emotions were a barrier to your success and much more. Completing all the fifteen auditing steps contained in this book sets you up for really being in *control* of your environment and life.

Child Dianetics • Here is a revolutionary new approach to rearing children with Dianetics auditing techniques. Find out how you can help your child achieve greater confidence, more self-reliance, improved learning rate and a happier, more loving relationship with you.

Notes on the Lectures of L. Ron Hubbard • Compiled from his fascinating lectures given shortly after the publication of *Dianetics*, this book contains some of the first material Ron ever released on the ARC tiangle and the Tone Scale, and how these discoveries relate to auditing.

Basic Dianetics Books

The Basic Dianetics Books Package is your complete guide to the inner workings of the mind. You can get all of these books individually or in a set, complete with an attractive slipcase.

Dianetics: The Modern Science of Mental Health • Acclaimed as the most effective self-help book ever published. Dianetics technology has helped millions reach new heights of freedom and ability. Millions of copies are sold every year! Discover the source of mental barriers that prevent you from achieving your goals—and how to handle them!

The Dynamics of Life • Break through the barriers to your happiness. This is the first book Ron wrote detailing the startling principles behind Dianetics—facts so powerful they can change forever the way you look at yourself and your potentials. Discover how you can use the powerful basic principles in this book to blast through the barriers of your mind and gain full control over your success, future and happiness.

Self Analysis • The complete do-it-yourself handbook for anyone who wants to improve their abilities and success potential. Use the simple, easy-to-learn techniques in *Self Analysis* to build self-confidence and reduce stress.

Dianetics: The Evolution of a Science • It is estimated that we use less than ten percent of our mind's potential. What stops us from developing and using the full potential of our minds? *Dianetics: The Evolution of a Science* is L. Ron Hubbard's incredible story of how he discovered the reactive mind and how he developed the keys to unlock its secrets. Get this firsthand account of what the mind really is, and how you can release its hidden potential.

Basic Scientology Books

The Basic Scientology Books Package contains the knowledge you need to be able to improve conditions in life. These books are available individually or as a set, complete with an attractive slipcase.

Scientology: The Fundamentals of Thought • Improve life *and* make a better world with this easy-to-read book that lays out the fundamental truths about life and thought. No such knowledge has ever before existed, and no such results have ever before been attainable as those which can be reached by the use of this knowledge. Equipped with this book alone, one could perform seeming miracles in changing the states of health, ability and intelligence of people. This *is* how life works. This *is* how you change men, women and children for the better, and attain greater personal freedom.

A New Slant on Life • Have you ever asked yourself, Who am I? What am I? This book of articles by L. Ron Hubbard answers these all too common questions. This is knowledge one can use everyday—for a new, more confident and happier slant on life!

The Problems of Work • Work plays a big part in the game of life. Do you really enjoy your work? Are you certain of your job security? Would you like the increased personal satisfaction of doing your work well? This is the book that shows exactly how to achieve these things and more. The game of life—and within it, the game of work—can be enjoyable and rewarding.

Scientology 0-8: The Book of Basics • What is life? Did you know an individual can create space, energy and time? Here are the basics of life itself, and the secrets of becoming cause over any area of your life. Discover how you can use the data in this book to achieve your goals.

Other Scientology Books

Scientology 8-80 • What are the laws of life? We are all familiar with physical laws such as the law of gravity, but what laws govern life and thought? L. Ron Hubbard answers the riddles of life and its goals in the physical universe.

Scientology 8-8008 • Get the basic truths about your nature as a spiritual being and your relationship to the physical universe around you. Here, L. Ron Hubbard describes procedures designed to increase your abilities to heights previously only dreamed of.

Scientology: A History of Man • A fascinating look at the evolutionary background and history of the human race. This was Ron's first book on the vast time track of man. As Ron said, "This is a cold-blooded and factual account of your last sixty trillion years."

The Creation of Human Ability • This book contains processes designed to restore the power of a theta over his own postulates, to understand the nature of his beingness, to free his self-determinism and much, much more.

The Phoenix Lectures • Containing L. Ron Hubbard's most complete discussion of the Scientology Axioms, *The Phoenix Lectures* gives you the full knowledge of the basic agreements which make up the very nature of the universe we live in.

Purification: An Illustrated Answer to Drugs • Do toxins and drugs hold down your ability to think clearly? What is the Purification Program and how does it work? How can harmful chemical substances be gotten out of the body? Our society is ridden by abuse of drugs, alcohol and medicine that reduce one's ability to think clearly. Find out what can be done in this introduction to the Purification Program.

All About Radiation • Can the effects of radiation exposure be avoided or reduced? What exactly would happen in the event of an atomic explosion? Get the answers to these and many other questions in this illuminating book. *All About Radiation* describes observations and discoveries concerning the physical and mental effects of radiation and the possibilities for handling them. Get the real facts on the subject of radiation and its effects.

Have You Lived Before This Life? • This is the book that sparked a flood of interest in the ancient puzzle: Does man live only one life? The answer lay in mystery, buried until L. Ron

Hubbard's researches unearthed the truth. Actual case histories of people recalling past lives in auditing tell the tale.

The following books on the E-Meter give all the data you need to understand and professionally operate your E-Meter. You can get all of these books individually or in a set, complete with an attractive slipcase.

Introducing the E-Meter • This is a basic book that introduces you to the E-Meter spiritual counseling device and its operation.

Understanding the E-Meter • A large, illustrated book that fully explains the basics of the E-Meter device, how it works and how it can measure the electrical activity of thought. Any question on the principles of the E-Meter can be answered with this book.

E-Meter Essentials • This book gives more advanced aspects of E-Meter use, plus a detailed description of the different types of meter reads on the meter and what they mean.

The Book of E-Meter Drills • With this book you learn all phases of E-Meter operation with detailed, hands-on drills.

Mission Into Time • Here is a fascinating account of a unique research expedition into both space and time, locating physical evidence of past lives in an area rich with history—the Mediterranean. Read Ron's story of the exploration of locations recalled from previous lives!

Basic Dictionary of Dianetics and Scientology • Compiled from the works of L. Ron Hubbard, this convenient dictionary contains the terms and expressions needed by anyone learning Dianetics and Scientology technology. And a *special bonus*—an easy-to-read Scientology Organizing Board chart that shows you who to contact for services and information at your nearest Scientology Organization.

Dianetics and Scientology Technical Dictionary • This dictionary is your indispensable guide to the words and ideas of Scientology and Dianetics technologies—technologies which can help you increase your know-how and effectiveness in life. Over three thousand words are defined—including a new understanding of vital words like *life, love* and *happiness* as well as Scientology terms.

Modern Management Technology Defined: Hubbard Dictionary of Administration and Management • Here's a real breakthrough in the subject of administration and management! Eighty-six hundred words are defined for greater understanding of any business situation. Clear, precise Scientology definitions describe many previously baffling phenomena and bring truth, sanity and understanding to the often murky field of business management.

How to Live Though an Executive • What are the factors in business and commerce which, if lacking, can keep a person overworked and worried, keep labor and management at each other's throats, and make an unsafe working atmosphere? L. Ron Hubbard reveals principles based on years of research into many different types of organizations.

Introduction to Scientology Ethics • A complete knowledge of ethics is vital to anyone's success in life. Without knowing and applying the information in this book, success is only a matter of luck or chance. That is not much to look forward to. This book contains the answers to questions like, "How do I know when a decision is right or wrong?" "How can I predictably improve things around me?" The powerful ethics technology of L. Ron Hubbard is your way to ever-increasing survival.

Organization Executive Course • The *Organization Executive Course* volumes contain organizational technology never before known to man. This is not just how a Scientology organization works; this is how the operation of *any* organization, *any* activity, can be improved. A person knowing the data in these volumes fully, and applying it, could completely reverse any downtrend in a company—or even a country!

Management Series Volumes 1 and 2 • These books contain technology that anyone who works with management in any way must know completely to be a true success. Contained in these books are such subjects as data evaluation, the technology of how to organize any area for maximum production and expansion, how to handle personnel, the actual technology of public relations and much more.

Background and Ceremonies of the Church of Scientology • Discover the beautiful and inspiring ceremonies of the Church of Scientology, and its fascinating religious and historical background. This book contains the illuminating Creed of the Church, church services, sermons and ceremonies, many as originally given in person by L. Ron Hubbard, Founder of Scientology.

What Is Scientology? • Scientology applied religious philosophy has attracted great interest and attention since its beginning. What is Scientology philosophy? What can it accomplish— and why are so many people from all walks of life proclaiming its effectiveness? Find the answers to these questions and many others in *What Is Scientology?*

Introductory and Demonstration Processes and Assists • How can you help someone increase his enthusiasm for living?

How can you improve someone's self-confidence on the job? Here are basic Scientology processes you can use to help others deal with life and living.

Volunteer Minister's Handbook • This is a big, practical how-to-do-it book to give a person the basic knowledge on how to help self and others through the rough spots in life. It consists of twenty-one sections—each one covering important situations in life, such as drug and alcohol problems, study difficulties, broken marriages, accidents and illnesses, a failing business, difficult children, and much more. This is the basic tool you need to help someone out of troubles, and bring about a happier life.

Research and Discovery Series • These volumes contain only existing day-to-day, week-to-week record of the progress of L. Ron Hubbard's research in Dianetics and Scientology. Through the pages of these beautiful volumes you follow L. Ron Hubbard's fantastic research adventure, beginning in the depths of man's degradation and obsession with the material universe and soaring to the realms of the spirit, freed from the bondage of the past.

Technical Bulletins • These volumes contain all of L. Ron Hubbard's technical bulletins and issues from the earliest to the latest. Almost any technical question can be answered from the pages of these volumes, which also include an extremely extensive master subject index.

The Classic Cassettes Series

There are nearly three thousand recorded lectures by L. Ron Hubbard on the subjects of Dianetics and Scientology. What follows is a sampling of these lectures, each known and loved the world over. All of the Classic Cassettes are presented in Clearsound state-of-the-art sound-recording technology, notable for its clarity and brilliance of reproduction.

The Story of Dianetics and Scientology • In this lecture, L. Ron Hubbard shares with you his earliest insights into human nature and gives a compelling and often humorous account of his experiences. Spend an unforgettable time with Ron as he talks about the start of Dianetics and Scientology!

The Road to Truth • The road to truth has eluded man since the beginning of time. In this classic lecture, L. Ron Hubbard explains what this road actually is and why it is the only road one MUST travel all the way once begun. This lecture reveals the only road to higher levels of living.

Scientology and Effective Knowledge • Voyage to new horizons of awareness! *Scientology and Effective Knowledge* by L. Ron Hubbard can help you understand more about yourself and others. A fascinating tale of the beginnings of Dianetics and Scientology.

The Deterioration of Liberty • What do governments fear so much in a population that they amass weapons to defend themselves from people? Find out from Ron in this classic lecture.

Man's Relentless Search • Learn about man's search for himself and his true nature. Find out where this search led and how through Ron's work we have achieved a knowledge of man's true self.

Power of Choice and Self-Determinism • Man's ability to determine the course of his life depends on his ability to exercise his power of choice. Find how you can increase your power of choice and self-determinism in life from Ron in this lecture.

Scientology and Ability • Ron points out that this universe is here because we perceive it and agree to it. Applying Scientology principles to life can bring new adventure to life and put you on the road to discovering better beingness.

The Road to Perfection • Find out what perfection really is and how Scientology gives you the means to attain it.

The Dynamics • In this lecture Ron gives incredible data on the dynamics: how man creates on them, what happens when a person gets stuck in just one; how wars relate to the third dynamic and much more.

Health and Certainty • Ron talks in this classic lecture about the effect false certainty can bring about in an individual and how real certainty is achieved.

Miracles • What are miracles? How do they come about? Find out how things that used to pass as miracles have become just the expected results of Dianetics and Scientology.

My Philosophy • Three dramatic essays by Ron—"My Philosophy," "The Aims of Scientology" and "A Description of Scientology"—come alive for you in this cassette. These powerful writings, beautifully read and set to new and inspiring music, tell you what Scientology is, what it does and what its aims are.

More advanced books and lectures are available. Contact your nearest organization or write directly to the publisher for a full catalog.

Improve Your Life with Dianetics Graduate Extension Courses

Dianetics Graduate books by L. Ron Hubbard give you the knowledge of how the mind works and how you can use that data to help yourself and others to break out of the traps of life. The Dianetics Graduate Extension courses enable you to increase your application of the information contained in L. Ron Hubbard's books and make this a saner world for all.

Each extension course package includes a lesson book with easy-to-understand instructions and all the lessons you will need to complete it. Each course can be done in the comfort of your own home or right in your local Scientology organization. Your Extension Course Supervisor will review each lesson as you complete it (or mail it in if you do the course at home) and get the results right back to you. When you complete the course you get a beautiful certificate, suitable for framing.

Dianetics 55! Extension Course

Dianetics 55! forms an excellent bridge from the study of the mind to the study of knowledge in its fullest sense—Scientology. Doing the extension course for this book can help you grasp the tremendous amount of important data it contains so you can better apply this information to your benefit. Start today by enrolling on the *Dianetics 55! Extension Course.*

Science of Survival Extension Course

Science of Survival was written around a remarkable chart that lays out all the characteristics of human behavior—the Hubbard Chart of Human Evaluation. To learn more about what lies behind the emotional tone levels of others, how you predict how they will react and how to handle them, do the *Science of Survival Extension Course!*

Advanced Procedure and Axioms Extension Course

For the *first* time the basics of thought and the physical universe have been codified into a set of fundamental laws, signaling an entirely new way to view and approach the subjects of man, the physical universe and even life itself. Gain a full understanding of postulates, self-determinism and *full* responsibility on the *Advanced Procedure and Axioms Extension Course.*

Handbook for Preclears Extension Course

L. Ron Hubbard wrote this book in 1951 in response to the need for an advanced personal workbook. People who follow the exact steps laid out in this book achieve definite, positive changes in the conditions in their lives. Find out what you CAN do about the conditions in your life.

Child Dianetics Extension Course

In 1951 Ron wrote in the introduction to *Child Dianetics*:

"The American Medical Association lately came out with a pamphlet which was called 'How to Control Your Child.' That's just what you don't want to do."

There *is* a correct way to have a successful relationship with children. Enroll on the *Child Dianetics Extension Course* and learn the workable way to get healthy, happier and more successful children. A "must" for any parent or teacher.

The Notes on the Lectures Extension Course

The physical universe and the universe of thought are two different universes that can have profound effects on an individual's ability to survive or succumb. Learn how Dianetics processing works to bring a person up out of the turbulence of the physical universe to the point of being able to create in life, on all dynamics. Find out more about people—why they are what they are.

Enroll on a Dianetics Graduate Extension Course Today!

For information and enrollment and prices for these Extension Courses and the books they accompany, contact the Public Registrar at your nearest Church of Scientology. (A complete list of Scientology Churches and Organizations is provided at the back of this book.)

Get and start a Dianetics Graduate Extension Course today!

Get Your Free Catalog
of Knowledge on
How to Improve Life

L. Ron Hubbard's books and tapes increase your ability to understand yourself and others. His works give you the practical know-how you need to improve your life and the lives of your family and friends.

Many more materials by L. Ron Hubbard are available than have been covered in the pages of this book. A free catalog of these materials is available on request.

Write for your free catalog today!

Bridge Publications, Inc.
4751 Fountain Avenue
Los Angeles, California 90029

New Era Publications International, ApS
Store Kongensgade 55
1264 Copenhagen K, Denmark

Apply for Your International Association Membership Today!

The recently created International Association of Scientologists invites you to apply for your annual or lifetime membership today.

The purpose of the International Association of Scientologists is:

"to unite, advance, support and protect Scientology and Scientologists in all parts of the world so as to achieve the aims and purposes of Scientology."

Benefits extended to International Association members include:

* The right to be awarded and hold in force certificates for Scientology and Dianetics training, internship and processing services successfully completed
* Eligibility for professional rates on processing services
* Eligibility for training scholarship awards
* Eligibility for appointment as a Field Staff Member
* Special rates on membership fees for the "I Want to Go OT" Club
* Special rates on Dianetics and Scientology materials and services —including a 20 percent discount on books, tapes and E-Meters.

These benefits are now available only to members of the International Association of Scientologists.

A free six-month membership is extended to beginning Scientologists only—those buying their first book or their first training or processing service.

Apply to the Membership Officer at your nearest Church of Scientology today. Or write directly to the *International Association of Scientologists*, c/o Saint Hill Manor, East Grinstead, Sussex, England RH19 4JY.

"I am always happy to hear from my readers."

L. Ron Hubbard

These were the words of L. Ron Hubbard, who was always very interested in hearing from his friends and readers. He made a point of staying in communication with everyone he came in contact with over his fifty-year career as a professional writer, and he had thousands of fans and friends that he corresponded with all over the world.

The publishers of L. Ron Hubbard's works wish to continue this tradition and welcome letters and comments from you, his readers, both old and new.

Additionally, the publishers will be happy to send you information on anything you would like to know about Ron, his extraordinary life and accomplishments and the vast number of books he has written.

Any message addressed to the Author's Affairs Director at Bridge Publications will be given prompt and full attention.

Bridge Publications, Inc.
4751 Fountain Avenue
Los Angeles, California 90029
U.S.A.

Church and Organization Address List

Las Vegas *(cont.)*
Church of Scientology
Celebrity Centre Las Vegas
1100 South 10th Street
Las Vegas, Nevada 89104

Long Island
Church of Scientology
330 Fulton Avenue
Hempstead, New York 11550

Los Angeles and vicinity
Church of Scientology
4810 Sunset Boulevard
Los Angeles, California 90027

Church of Scientology
1451 Irvine Boulevard
Tustin, California 92680

Church of Scientology
263 East Colorado Boulevard
Pasadena, California 91101

Church of Scientology
10335 Magnolia Boulevard
North Hollywood, California 91601

Church of Scientology
American Saint Hill Organization
1413 North Berendo Street
Los Angeles, California 90027

Church of Scientology
American Saint Hill Foundation
1413 North Berendo Street
Los Angeles, California 90027

Church of Scientology
Advanced Organization of
  Los Angeles
1306 North Berendo Street
Los Angeles, California 90027

Church of Scientology
Celebrity Centre International
5930 Franklin Avenue
Hollywood, California 90028

Miami
Church of Scientology
120 Giralda Avenue
Coral Gables, Florida 33134

Minneapolis
Church of Scientology
3019 Minnehaha Avenue
Minneapolis, Minnesota 55406

New Haven
Church of Scientology
909 Whalley Avenue
New Haven, Connecticut 06515

New York City
Church of Scientology
227 West 46th Street
New York City, New York 10036

Church of Scientology
Celebrity Centre New York
65 East 82nd Street
New York City, New York 10028

Orlando
Church of Scientology
710-A East Colonial Drive
Orlando, Florida 32803

Philadelphia
Church of Scientology
1315 Race Street
Philadelphia, Pennsylvania 19107

Phoenix
Church of Scientology
4450 North Central Avenue, Suite 102
Phoenix, Arizona 85012

Portland
Church of Scientology
1536 Southeast 11th Avenue
Portland, Oregon 97214

Church of Scientology
Celebrity Centre Portland
709 Southwest Salmon Street
Portland, Oregon 97205

Sacramento
Church of Scientology
825 15th Street
Sacramento, California 95814

San Diego
Church of Scientology
701 "C" Street
San Diego, California 92101

San Francisco
Church of Scientology
83 McAllister Street
San Francisco, California 94102

San Jose
Church of Scientology
3604 Stevens Creek Boulevard
San Jose, California 95117

Santa Barbara
Church of Scientology
524 State Street
Santa Barbara, California 93101

Seattle
Church of Scientology
2004 Westlake Avenue
Seattle, Washington 98121

St. Louis
Church of Scientology
9510 Page Boulevard
St. Louis, Missouri 63132

Tampa
Church of Scientology
4809 North Armenia Avenue, Suite 215
Tampa, Florida 33603

Clearwater
Church of Scientology
Flag® Service Organization
210 South Fort Harrison Avenue
Clearwater, Florida 33516

Washington, DC
Founding Church of Scientology
2125 "S" Street NW
Washington, DC 20008

Canada

Edmonton
Church of Scientology
10349 82nd Avenue
Edmonton, Alberta
Canada T6E 1Z9

Kitchener
Church of Scientology
8 Water Street North
Kitchener, Ontario
Canada N2H 5A5

Montreal
Church of Scientology
4489 Papineau Street
Montréal, Québec
Canada H2H 1T7

Ottawa
Church of Scientology
150 Rideau Street, 2nd Floor
Ottawa, Ontario
Canada K1N 5X6

Quebec
Church of Scientology
226 St-Joseph est
Québec, Québec
Canada G1K 3A9

Toronto
Church of Scientology
696 Yonge Street
Toronto, Ontario
Canada M4Y 2A7

Vancouver
Church of Scientology
401 West Hastings Street
Vancouver, British Columbia
Canada V6B 1L5

Winnipeg
Church of Scientology
Suite 125—388 Donald Street
Winnipeg, Manitoba
Canada R3B 2J4

United Kingdom

Birmingham
Church of Scientology
80 Hurst Street
Birmingham
England B5 4TD

Brighton
Church of Scientology
Dukes Arcade, Top Floor
Dukes Street
Brighton, Sussex
England

East Grinstead
Saint Hill Foundation
Saint Hill Manor
East Grinstead, West Sussex
England RH19 4JY

Advanced Organization Saint Hill
Saint Hill Manor
East Grinstead, West Sussex
England RH19 4JY

Edinburgh
Hubbard Academy of Personal
  Independence
20 Southbridge
Edinburgh, Scotland EH1 1LL

London
Church of Scientology
68 Tottenham Court Road
London, W1P 0BB England

Manchester
Church of Scientology
258 Deansgate
Manchester, England M3 4BG

Plymouth
Church of Scientology
41 Ebrington Street
Plymouth, Devon
England PL4 9AA

Sunderland
Church of Scientology
51 Fawcett Street
Sunderland, Tyne and Wear
England SR1 1RS

Austria

Vienna
Church of Scientology
Mariahilfer Strasse 88A/II/2
A-1070 Vienna, Austria

Belgium

Brussels
Church of Scientology
45A, rue de l'Ecuyer
1000 Bruxelles, Belgium

Denmark

Aarhus
Church of Scientology
Guldsmedegade 17, 2
8000 Aarhus C, Denmark

Copenhagen
Church of Scientology
Store Kongensgade 55
1264 Copenhagen K, Denmark

Church of Scientology
Vesterbrogade 23 A – 25
1620 Copenhagen V, Denmark

Church of Scientology
Advanced Organization Saint Hill for
  Europe and Africa
Jernbanegade 6
1608 Copenhagen V, Denmark

France

Angers
Church of Scientology
10–12, rue Max Richard
49000 Angers, France

Clermont-Ferrand
Church of Scientology
2 Pte rue Giscard de la Tour Fondue
63000 Clermont-Ferrand, France

Lyon
Church of Scientology
3, place des Capucins
69001 Lyon, France

Paris
Church of Scientology
65, rue de Dunkerque
75009 Paris, France

Church of Scientology
Celebrity Centre Paris
69, rue Legendre
75017 Paris, France

St. Etienne
Church of Scientology
24, rue Marengo
42000 St. Etienne, France

Germany

Berlin
Church of Scientology e.V.
Sponholzstrasse 51/52
1000 Berlin 41, Germany

Düsseldorf
Church of Scientology
Friedrichstrasse 28
4000 Düsseldorf, West Germany

Frankfurt
Church of Scientology
Darmstadter Landstr. 119–125
6000 Frankfurt/Main, West Germany

Hamburg
Church of Scientology e.V.
Steindamm 63
2000 Hamburg 1, West Germany

Church of Scientology
Celebrity Centre Hamburg
Mönckebergstrasse 5
2000 Hamburg 1
West Germany

Munich
Church of Scientology e.V.
Beichstrasse 12
D-8000 München 40, West Germany

Greece

Athens
Applied Philosophy Center of Greece
(K.E.F.E.)
Ippokratous 175B
114 72 Athens, Greece

Israel

Tel Aviv
Scientology and Dianetics College
7 Salomon Street
Tel Aviv 66023, Israel

Italy

Brescia
Church of Scientology
Dei Tre Laghi
Via Fratelli Bronzetti N. 20
25125 Brescia, Italy

Milano
Church of Scientology
Via Abetone, 10
20137 Milano, Italy

Monza
Church of Scientology
Via Cavour, 5
20052 Monza, Italy

Novara
Church of Scientology
Corso Cavallotti No. 7
28100 Novara, Italy

Nuoro
Church of Scientology
Corso Garibaldi, 108
08100 Nuoro, Italy

Padua
Church of Scientology
Via Mameli 1/5
35131 Padova, Italy

Pordenone
Church of Scientology
Via Montereale, 10/C
33170 Pordenone, Italy

Rome
Church of Scientology
Via di San Vito, 11
00185 Roma, Italy

Turin
Church of Scientology
Via Guarini, 4
10121 Torino, Italy

Verona
Church of Scientology
Vicolo Chiodo No. 4/A
37121 Verona, Italy

Netherlands

Amsterdam
Church of Scientology
Nieuwe Zijds Voorburgwal 271
1012 RL Amsterdam, Netherlands

Norway

Oslo
Church of Scientology
Storgata 9
0155 Oslo 1, Norway

Portugal

Lisbon
Instituto de Dianética
Rua Actor Taborde 39–4°
1000 Lisboa, Portugal

Spain

Barcelona
Dianética
Calle Pau Claris 85, Principal 1ª
08010 Barcelona, Spain

Madrid
Asociación Civil de Dianética
Montera 20, Piso 2
28013 Madrid, Spain

Sweden

Göteborg
Church of Scientology
Norra Hamngatan 4
S-411 14 Göteborg, Sweden

Malmö
Church of Scientology
Stortorget 27
S-211 34 Malmö, Sweden

Stockholm
Church of Scientology
Kammakargatan 46
S-111 60 Stockholm, Sweden

Switzerland

Basel
Church of Scientology
Herrengrabenweg 56
4054 Basel, Switzerland

Bern
Church of Scientology
Effingerstrasse 25
CH-3008 Bern, Switzerland

Geneva
Church of Scientology
4, rue du Léman
1201 Genève, Switzerland

Lausanne
Church of Scientology
10, rue de la Madeleine
1003 Lausanne, Switzerland

Zurich
Church of Scientology
Badenerstrasse 294
CH-8004 Zürich, Switzerland

Australia

Adelaide
Church of Scientology
24 Waymouth Street
Adelaide, South Australia 5000
Australia

Brisbane
Church of Scientology
2nd Floor, 106 Edward Street
Brisbane, Queensland 4000
Australia

Canberra
Church of Scientology
Suite 16, 108 Bunda Street
Canberra Civic
A.C.T 2601, Australia

Melbourne
Church of Scientology
44 Russell Street
Melbourne, Victoria 3000
Australia

Perth
Church of Scientology
39–41 King Street
Perth, Western Australia 6000
Australia

Sydney
Church of Scientology
201 Castlereagh Street
Sydney, New South Wales 2000
Australia

Church of Scientology
Advanced Organization Saint Hill
  Australia, New Zealand and
  Oceania
19–37 Greek Street
Glebe, New South Wales 2037
Australia

Japan

Tokyo
Scientology Tokyo Org
101 Toyomi Nishi Gotanda Heights
2-13-5 Nishi Gotanda
Shinagawa-Ku
Tokyo, Japan 141

New Zealand

Auckland
Church of Scientology
2nd Floor, 44 Queen Street
Auckland 1, New Zealand

Africa

Bulawayo
Church of Scientology
74 Abercorn Street
Bulawayo, Zimbabwe

Cape Town
Church of Scientology
5 Beckham Street
Gardens
Cape Town 8001, South Africa

Durban
Church of Scientology
57 College Lane
Durban 4001, South Africa

Harare
Church of Scientology
First Floor State Lottery Building
P.O. Box 3524
Corner Speke Avenue and
   Julius Nyerere Way
Harare, Zimbabwe

Johannesburg
Church of Scientology
Security Building, 2nd Floor
95 Commissioner Street
Johannesburg 2001, South Africa

Church of Scientology
101 Huntford Building
40 Hunter Street
Cnr. Hunter & Fortesque Roads
Yeoville 2198
Johannesburg, South Africa

Port Elizabeth
Church of Scientology
2 St. Christopher
27 Westbourne Road
Port Elizabeth 6001, South Africa

Pretoria
Church of Scientology
"Die Meent Arcade," 2nd Level,
   Shop 43b
266 Pretorius Street
Pretoria 0002, South Africa

Latin America

Colombia

Bogotá
Centro Cultural de Dianética
Carrera 19 No. 39–55
Apartado Aereo 92419
Bogotá, D.E. Colombia

Mexico

Estado de México
Instituto Tecnologico de Dianética,
   A.C.
Reforma 530, Lomas
México D.F., C.P. 11000

Guadalajara
Organización Cultural Dianética de
   Guadalajara, A.C.
Av. Lopez Mateos Nte. 329
Sector Hidalgo
Guadalajara, Jalisco, México

Mexico City
Asociación Cultural Dianética, A.C.
Hermes No. 46
Colonia Crédito Constructor
03940 México 19, D.F.

Instituto de Filosofia Aplicada, A.C.
Durango #105
Colonia Roma
06700 México D.F.

Instituto de Filosofia Aplicada, A.C.
Plaza Rio de Janeiro No. 52
Colonia Roma
06700 México D.F.

Organización, Desarrollo y
   Dianética, A.C.
Providencia 1000
Colonia Del Valle
C.P. 03100 México D.F.

Centro de Dianética Polanco
Insurgentes Sur 536, 1er piso
   Esq. Nogales
Colonia Roma Sur C.P.
06700 México D.F.

Venezuela

Valencia
Asociación Cultural Dianética de
   Venezuela, A.C.
Ave. 101 No. 150–23
Urbanizacion La Alegria
Apartado Postal 833
Valencia, Venezuela

To obtain any books or cassettes by L. Ron Hubbard which are not available at your local organization, contact any of the following publishers:

Bridge Publications, Inc.
4751 Fountain Avenue
Los Angeles, California 90029

Continental Publications Liaison Office
696 Yonge Street
Toronto, Ontario
Canada M4Y 2A7

New Era Publications International
 ApS
Store Kongensgade 55
1264 Copenhagen K, Denmark

Era Dinámica Editores, S.A. de C.V.
Alabama 105
Colonia Nápoles
C.P. 03810 México, D.F.

NEW ERA Publications, Ltd.
78 Holmethorpe Avenue
Redhill, Surrey RH1 2NL
United Kingdom

N.E. Publications Australia Pty. Ltd.
2 Verona Street
Paddington, New South Wales 2021
Australia

Continental Publications Pty. Ltd.
P.O. Box 27080
Benrose 2011
South Africa

NEW ERA Publications Italia Srl
Via L.G. Columella, 12
20128 Milano, Italy

NEW ERA Publications GmbH
Otto—Hahn—Strasse 25
6072 Dreieich 1, Germany

NEW ERA Publications France
111, Boulevard de Magenta
75010 Paris, France

New Era Publications España, S.A.
C/De la Paz, 4/1° dcha
28012 Madrid, Spain

New Era Japan
5-4-5-803 Nishigotanda
Shinagawa-Ku
Tokyo, Japan 141